# — THE —
# PIKE
# ANGLER'S
# MANUAL

## Barrie Rickards
## & Martin Gay

A & C Black • London

First published 1987 by
A & C Black (Publishers) Limited
35 Bedford Row, London WC1R 4JH

© 1987 Barrie Rickards and Martin Gay

ISBN 0 7136 5558 5

Rickards, Barrie
  The pike angler's manual.
  1. Pike fishing.
  I. Title  II. Gay, Martin
  799.1'753        SH691.P6

  ISBN 0–7136–5558–5

Printed and bound in Great Britain by
Hollen Street Press Limited,
Slough, Berkshire

# CONTENTS

# FOREWORD

When Martin Gay and Barrie Rickards asked me to write the introduction to this splendid treatise on the technical aspects of pike angling I felt both pleased and honoured. Just thinking about it caused my mind to drift back in time to the beginning of my own pike fishing career.

It started in the 1960s. I had not fished for pike before I moved to Norfolk, but I always knew I would do, one day. I was inspired by the Dennis Pye legend, long before I met the man. There is little doubt that he was a key figure in the development of pike angling, despite today's thoughts about his record. However, nobody really knows what he caught, and it no longer matters. He certainly took more and better fish than is now possible for most of us, and he was the first of many generous and kindly men I have been fortunate to encounter on the pike scene.

I happily fished with Dennis and some of the other Broadland greats, occasionally managing to snatch the odd crumb from their table! And then it was suddenly over. I had to leave Norfolk. Later that same year the vital Upper Thurne area died overnight, and strong men wept.

It took me several years to come to terms with pike fishing again. When you begin at the top, in that once lovely wilderness of reed and water, everything else can seem second-best, and I couldn't take it. I became very much a part-time piker for a while, though I took great care to keep in touch.

One of the ways I did that was to read nearly everything written on the subject by Barrie Rickards, and by Martin Gay who was very prolific at the time my piking career was in the abyss. From their writings alone I could read their characters—a gift which develops in those who write for a living—and my first impressions proved remarkably accurate when I eventually met them years later.

Martin I had marked down as rather shy and diffident. He looked that way in his photographs, but the quiet authority of his work gave the same indication. Martin did not dictate anything to anybody; you received a logical argument and sound reasons for what he was doing. I was disappointed when he suddenly stopped writing about pike, and I was keen to set him going again when I took charge of *Coarse Angler*. Happily, he obliged. I was also very pleased when his name appeared as a potential next President of the Pike Anglers' Club, and I was delighted when he accepted the position.

Barrie Rickards, a PAC founder and former Secretary, came over in his writing as a very different character—much more forceful, even abrasive at times. Barrie is trained to deal in hard fact, and I cannot remember him advancing a theory unless the evidence for it was already overwhelming.

For decades I doubt if any noted angling writer wrote anything without wondering what the great Richard Walker would make of it. In pike fishing Barrie has performed much the same function. Just the simple knowledge that he is there filters out some of the rubbish before it appears, but when somebody does get it wrong a response is virtually guaranteed. The innocent who strays out of line is gently corrected. The fool is sawn off from the limb on which he climbed out!

This is Walker's style to absolute perfection, but you cannot do it without knowing your subject inside out. The same relentless energy revealed in Barrie's writing is also applied to his fishing. By the time this appears he will probably have taken the thousandth double figure pike of his career—a truly formidable achievement.

I was present, with Martin, when Barrie landed his 980th (or whatever). It was the only fish on a hard but thoroughly enjoyable trip to Ardingly, which was soon to produce an amazing sequence of very big fish. Despite our lack of success they both predicted the bonanza to come. That Ardingly was special was simply shrieking at us from deep inside, and yet I knew I was going to blank on that occasion. I think Martin did, too.

This strange instinct of the experienced pike angler is impossible to explain, and it is almost as hard to define the extra qualities which separate good anglers from the exceptional ones. Whatever they are, Gay and Rickards have those gifts and few, if any, are as well qualified to put together a book of this kind.

Although they have not said it in so many words, I think one of their main motives has been to educate the angler into ways of enjoying the sport safely and sensibly. Respect for the pike and concern for its welfare are paramount considerations for both authors, and it has shaped their approach to the sport and the methods they employ.

I would like to thank them for their work; not just here, but in pike angling as a whole. They have done and are still doing valuable service, and we are beginning to see some of the benefits. They have helped to change the climate of opinion on pike preservation, and the situation at the aforementioned Ardingly could be seen as a major breakthrough. Here is a trout reservoir where the exceptional pike fishing is to be *protected*!

The message of the Pike Anglers' Club is getting through. That will be as much to the benefit of the pike fisher as the valuable information in this book. Reading *The Pike Angler's Manual* will make anyone a better pike angler, but the authors will think they have failed if you are not also convinced that there is more to the game than the mere catching of fish.

**Colin Dyson**

# RODS

Modern rod-building materials—carbon fibre, carbon/aramid fibre, boron and improved resin glass —have enabled pike rods to be increased in length to 11 and occasionally 12 feet. They still retain their lightness, crispness and an action which allows the angler to cast rather greater weights than those for which the 'blank' was designed. Pike anglers doubtless 'abuse' their rods more than any specialist angler casting large baits (often 4 to 6 oz), and yet they continue to expect a rod action which will enable a decent pike to give a good account of itself.

Test curves of between 2¼ and 3½ lb cover all pike fishing demands, coupled with lines of 11 to 15 lb b.s., but rod actions vary greatly. In recent years the tendency amongst rod designers, in addition to striving for lightness, has been towards 'fast' action rods. This design (Fig. a) is superb for casting leads considerable distances, that is *small, dense* weights, but it is less good in a pike fishing context for casting large deadbaits or livebaits which may be thrown from the hooks by the stiff butt. Fig. b shows the progressive action, the slow taper blank which, with its slow build-up of power, is ideal for livebaiting and for large deadbaits up to maximum casting ranges of around 80 yards. Where small deadbaits—sprats, sardines and smelt—and *lip* hooked livebaits are to be cast a long way (70 yards), with the aid of 2–4 oz leads, the fast taper design is definitely preferable.

Fibre glass performs well in slow taper rods, but carbon fibre, with its quicker recovery rate, is the preferred material with fast action rods.

The action of the blank dictates, to some extent, the ring spacing. Rings perform two main tasks: (1) they guide the line *out* on the cast and assist a smooth retrieve (and in this respect the more rings, the less friction, all other things being equal), and (2) they spread the load, or stress, along the blank as it bends into the cast, or into a fighting fish. Again, in theory at least, extra rings ease the loading along the rod, thereby lessening the friction on the line.

Fig. c details the standard ringing pattern where, for example, 9 or 10 rings are used on a rod of 11 feet, coned gradually towards the tip. Fig. d, the 'modern' arrangement, is used especially on fast action rods, where perhaps only 5 rings would be on that same 11-ft rod. Where fewer rings are utilised, the angle of the line across the inner surface of the ring can be such that when the rod is well bent the line runs across the ring *support*, rather than across the low friction 'wearing' surface. Modern rings—Fuji and Seymo—reduce line friction and so fewer can be used if wished; but few rings (5 or 6 on an 11- or 12-ft rod) mean an increase in resistance when 'pumping' in big fish, or a small weedbed, and a greater chance of line slap during the cast.

The length of the rod alone will not increase casting potential unless correct technique is used. An additional one or two feet will, however, assist when striking by picking up line more quickly, although the extra length may soften the action. The choice of a suitable length for a pike rod should relate to physical stature, but where this is difficult to judge we would suggest a length of 11 feet, a test curve of 2¾ to 3 lb and a slow or 'progressive' taper.

Rod fittings are clearly a matter of personal preference, but there are certain factors to consider. Where spigots are used to join the two (or more) sections, it is most important that a whipping is placed on the male *and* female sections, starting 2 mm from the end of each section and running to 15 mm on the male side, 25 mm on the female side. This strengthening may well prevent the section from splitting under load (see Fig. e).

Rings should be of a modern design using low friction materials, such as Fuji or Seymo. Both companies produce single and multi-leg rings and there is really little to choose under test except that the butt and second rings should always be 2 or 3 leg patterns, as the larger sizes need additional strengthening. Butt rings should have an inside diameter of 25 mm.

The rod handle (Fig. f) can be full length in cork or duplon, and as slim as the underlying blank permits. Most people find 15/16 inch O.D. most comfortable, but when the blank butt diameter is over-large, such as in a fast taper design, an abbreviated handle 6 inches in length must be permanently fixed—about 24 inches from the extreme butt end, and where the blank O.D. is usually around 1 inch (Fig. g). Again, cork or duplon may be used, especially if sliding winch fittings are chosen (see Fig. h).

Such fittings are usually perfectly adequate, except when a multiplier is used. Insufficient grip causes these reels to revolve slowly around the handle, although the John Roberts' patented winch fittings do overcome the problem. Alternatively, a Fuji reel clamp may be used (Fig. i). This pattern is fixed permanently to the rod and is whipped on a synthetic or cork 'sleeve', which acts as a buffer. Fuji also manufacture a screw winch fitting (FPS type); it is very light in weight, neat and functional and can be used, when fixed in position, on abbreviated or full length handles of any material.

Handle length and the position at which the reel is fixed are largely a matter of taste, and arm length, but most people find that a spacing of 20–23 inches from the butt end is the most comfortable. There is no virtue in overstretching oneself by placing the reel 30 inches along the rod—extra casting distance is not achieved and practical rod length is correspondingly reduced.

The very end of the rod handle needs some protection against damage on the ground, partly to protect the handle material but also the blank itself. A simple plastic or rubber cap is quite sufficient and it adds little weight.

## Rod Holdalls

A great many modern pike anglers, especially those who wear one-piece suits and rolled down waders, carry their rods tackled up, simply divided at the spigot, and the sections held together with rubber bands. Others carry their rods in individual cloth bags in a holdall, tackling up afresh each day. An increasing number of anglers use the roll-up holdall (on page 48) which was, in fact, 'invented' by Barrie in the late '60s. The rods are fully tackled up, with the exception of the reels which are removed, and the spools are tucked into the bottom pockets. The holdall does offer protection to the rods as each one is individually rolled in its own section of material. A well designed roll-up holdall should carry 4 or 5 rods, plus rod rests, landing net pole and umbrella. Commercially made models often carry outside pockets for the brolly and rod rests.

However, one word of warning. If you carry your rods tackled up, make sure you regularly re-tie knots and check the lines, as damage to both can easily occur.

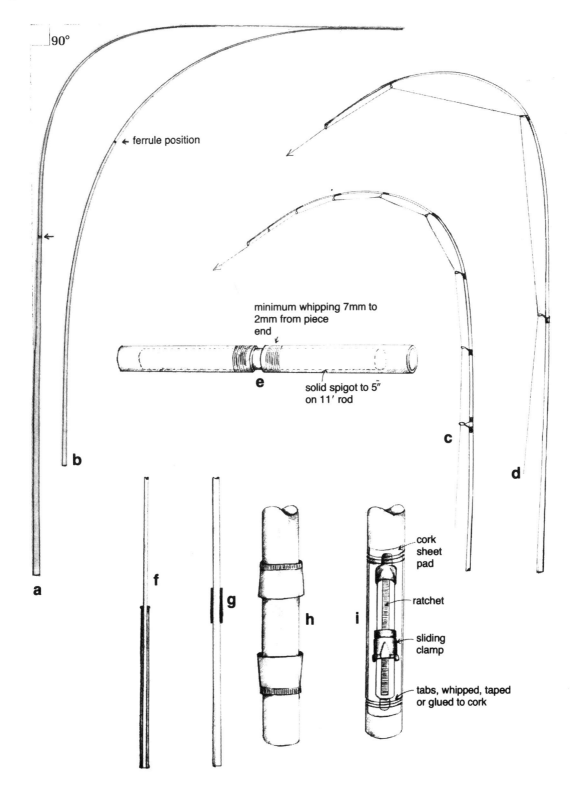

90°

← ferrule position

minimum whipping 7mm to 2mm from piece end

e

solid spigot to 5″ on 11′ rod

a    b    c    d    f    g    h    i

cork sheet pad

ratchet

sliding clamp

tabs, whipped, taped or glued to cork

# REELS

We cannot recommend that lines of less than 10 lb b.s. should ever be used in pike angling: one of 12 lb b.s. is far safer. This is not because absolute strength is needed to fight even a large pike (though it is a good enough reason), but mostly because of the rigours of casting heavy baits and the need, quite often, to bully big fish away from weeds and snags where they are regularly found.

Strong lines inevitably have a large diameter (12 lb b.s. Maxima is 0.32 mm), and this, coupled with the need to carry about 200 yards on the spool, necessitates the use of a robust reel. In turn, large spools invariably mean a powerful reel. Reliability and a line retrieve ratio of about 3·5:1 to give good winching power are probably the basic requirements of a piking reel. All are met, of course, by an open face fixed spool reel, and we would suggest that this design of reel is as far as the pike angler need look (see Figs 1a–c).

There is a certain charm in the use of multipliers (Fig. 2a), closed face fixed spool reels (Fig. 3) and centre pins (Fig. 4), and, indeed, there are small advantages individually. For example, because the line does not have to climb over the spool lip, and thereby does not increase resistance on longer casts, multipliers offer some advantage in long casting when strong lines are needed—say 15 lb b.s. However, to offset this, the slipping clutch of a multiplier is snatchy and of dubious reliability, and the line cannot be given by backwinding. For lure fishing some anglers find it easier to be accurate with a multiplier.

A large centre pin offers considerably greater line capacity than any freshwater sized fixed spool reel, and so wind assisted bait drifting can be executed at much greater range. But the absence of gearing makes all that rewinding of line (and hopefully a big pike!) extremely tedious. Long casting is also impossible with the centre pin. The 'sidecast' reel, as shown in Fig. 4b, is a hybrid centre pin in which the spool can be turned through 90° so that it faces up the rod. The spool lip resistance is thereby increased, though of course on most drains and some rivers this does not matter, and it can even improve the enjoyment of long trotting.

Where distance is not important, but accuracy is, the closed face fixed spool reel (Fig. 3) may offer some advantage, especially when used with a short 'bait casting' rod. Line capacity is poor, and line resistance before leaving the reel is high, so overall the reel has limited application in piking.

The above, therefore, are some of the considerations to bear in mind when selecting a pike reel, and almost every requirement is met with the open face fixed spool reel—the best-known and most widely used being the Mitchell 300 and 410 (the latter having a faster retrieve); Daiwa, Ryobi and Abu, amongst others, also produce good reels.

Long and trouble-free casting is easily achieved with a fixed spool reel, especially one with a wide spool as used exclusively on Mitchell reels. However, distance is attained only with a full spool as shown in Fig. 1a where the line is level with the spool lip. In Fig. 1b we show an incorrectly loaded spool where the line has 1/16 inch of spool lip to climb even before the cast is made, and valuable yards are lost immediately.

Multipliers will not cast light-weight baits as easily as the fixed spool reel, and attempting to do so is just one of the causes of overrun—the commonly seen 'bird's nest' (Fig. 2b). Snatchy casts, failure to feather the spool as the bait hits the water and incorrect spindle resistance setting are the other common causes. Multipliers really come into their own when long distance casting with heavy leads and small baits is called for.

The majority of multipliers are right-hand wind which, quite apart from being illogical, means that much hand changing is called for between casting and retrieving. Fortunately, Ryobi manufacture left-hand wind models, which is much in keeping with the predominance of left-hand wind fixed spool reels!

Clearly, line must be given to a strong running fish. Centre pins can yield line smoothly by allowing the spool to rotate backwards under pressure. Multipliers have inbuilt slipping clutches which can be adjusted to pull, but tend to be rather snatchy and can lock up without warning. Fixed spool reels also have slipping clutches adjusted either on the spool face or at the stern of the reel. Again, they can be unreliable and we much prefer to screw the clutch down tight and give line grudgingly by backwinding—which does not mean letting the handle spin freely backwards: it means turning the reel slowly backwards as the fish demands. In this way the whole fight is controlled and is controllable, and line is given only when absolutely necessary. Slipping clutches can cause line twist, backwind does not.

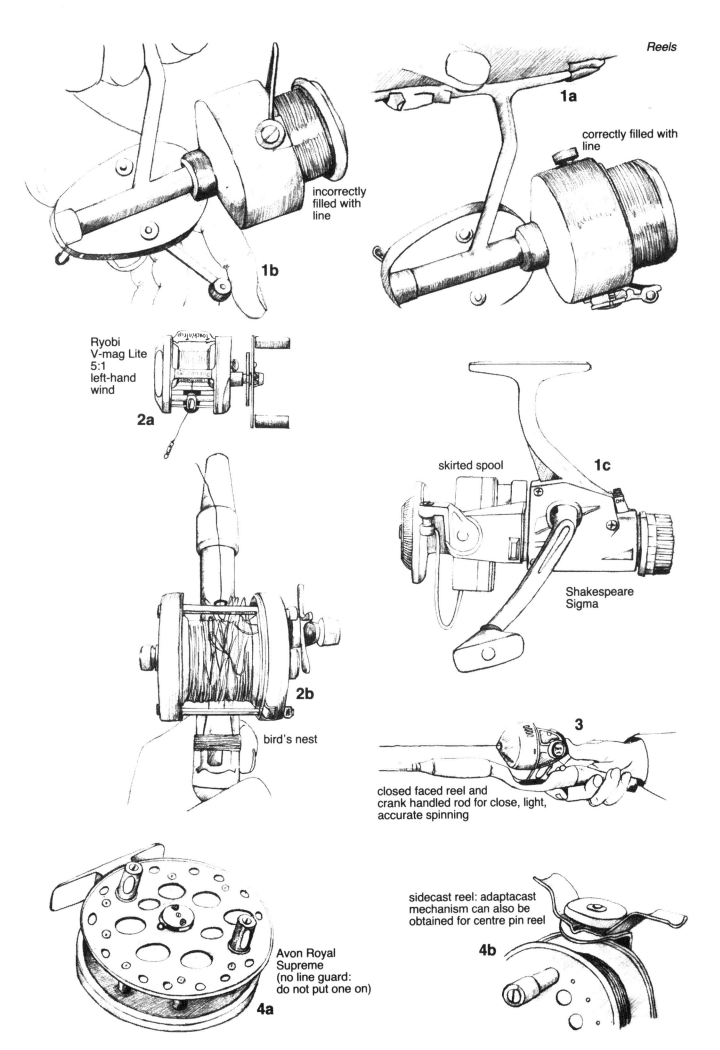

incorrectly
filled with
line

**1b**

**1a**

correctly filled with
line

Ryobi
V-mag Lite
5:1
left-hand
wind

**2a**

skirted spool

**1c**

Shakespeare
Sigma

**2b**

bird's nest

**3**

closed faced reel and
crank handled rod for close, light,
accurate spinning

Avon Royal
Supreme
(no line guard:
do not put one on)

**4a**

sidecast reel: adaptacast
mechanism can also be
obtained for centre pin reel

**4b**

# LINE AND TRACE WIRE ATTACHMENT

We use just *two* knots for all our piking and both are merely variations on the same theme. For attaching reel line to trace swivels, and fixed leads to paternoster links, we use the tucked half blood knot. Martin Gay, who employs Maxima almost exclusively, makes an 8-turn knot; Barrie Rickards is more adventurous in his selection of pike lines and adjusts the number of turns according to the brand of monofilament. For example, Platil *Standard* needs only 5 turns, the knot strength actually deteriorating after 6 turns, whereas Sylcast needs 6 or even 8 for maximum strength. Fig. 1a shows the basic knot before tightening, and Fig. 1b after pulling it tight. Always moisten the knot (with saliva or water) before pulling tight, as a dry knot can actually lose strength due to frictional heat.

Our pike lines usually have permanently attached stop knots. At one time Martin Gay merely tied a bunch of granny knots with ring whipping thread at the required point, but the unsatisfactory aspect of this has finally come home, and he has now joined Barrie Rickards in using the standard 'Billy Lane' sliding full blood knot. Figs 2a and 2b detail the knot, moistened before tightening. The two free ends should be trimmed to about ½ inch each—longer and they can cause line tangles, much shorter and the line snags on the cast.

A reliable trace wire is absolutely essential in piking, and people who recommend the use of nylon traces are inexperienced and are effectively advocating the leaving of hooks in pike. Pay no heed to them! Trace wire cannot safely be attached directly to nylon, which is primarily why swivels (and occasionally the less reliable split ring) are used on all pike traces. The swivel is tied to the reel line with the tucked half blood knot, but this knot cannot be used on wire.

The method by which we attach hooks and swivels to trace wire is simple and standard on all forms of stranded wire (the only type we recommend). Figs 3a–c illustrate the procedure which involves passing 2 inches of one end of the trace *twice* through the eye of the swivel (or hook), and then, under tension, twisting the free end *tightly* around the main trace, ensuring that each twist is butted firmly against its predecessor. Aim for about ½ inch of twists, the result being thoroughly reliable, neat and practical. There is no need for solder blobs or 'superglue' as the coils cannot untwist.

Wire is, of course, used in pike traces to prevent the fish biting off the terminal tackle and, with care, traces will last a number of outings. Weak spots can occur, however, at points where Ryder hooks are moved along the trace, leading to physical damage and rusting, and at sharply angled points when hooks are rigidly fixed. By far the commonest cause of failure is kinking of the trace, often during the cast. Sometimes the bait loops back 'over itself' forming a circle (Fig. 4a) which, when drawn tight, makes the kink (Fig. 4b). Kinks are *always* weak spots and the trace must be discarded. Just as hazardous is that shown in Fig. 4c where one, or more, of the 5–7 strands which comprise the wire is broken, leading to reduced strength. Rusting can also produce weakness and is the third common cause of trace failure. It is absolutely essential that regular checks are made at hook and swivel attachment points and along the length of the trace. If anything looks suspect, discard the trace. Take no chances on this crucial link between fish and angler.

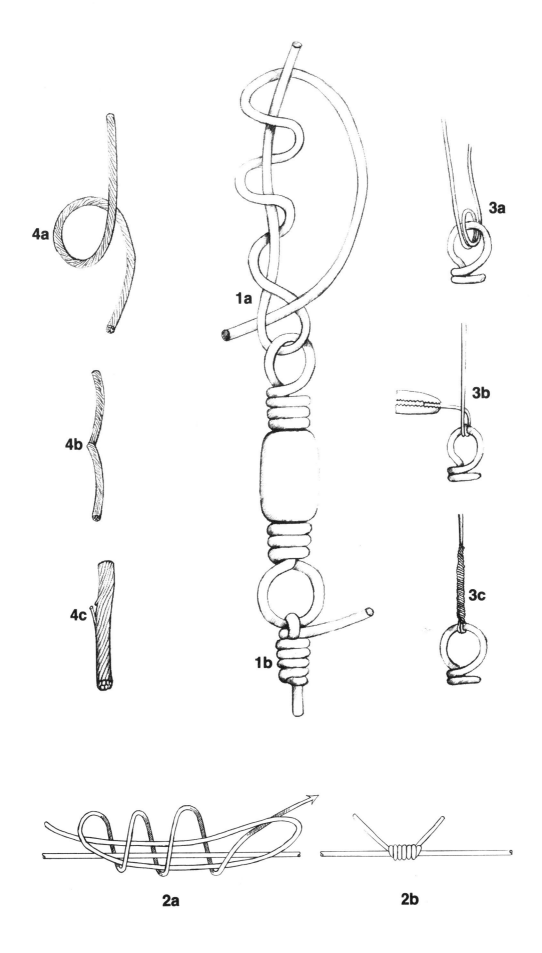

**4a**

**4b**

**4c**

**1a**

**1b**

**3a**

**3b**

**3c**

**2a**

**2b**

# HOOKS

The modern pike angler is keenly aware that carefully designed rigs, with small neat hooks, are just as important for the successful hooking of pike as the pike's uninjured return is for the future of fishery stocks. These two factors have led many anglers to choose barbless hooks (both singles and trebles), and in some cases to the exclusive use of single hooks for all their pike fishing.

There is no doubt that this trend enables hooks to be removed particularly easily, which is good for the pike. However, simple hook removal can also be achieved by quick striking, the use of sensibly small baits and time-proven unhooking techniques. Single hooks can, in special circumstances, prove as efficient as trebles—small live and deadbaits which can be liphooked, for example—though we believe it is a mistake to use them with all bait types and techniques. Large and/or soft deadbaits can occasionally mask the hook point, resulting in a missed strike—a situation which calls for the hook to stand proud of the bait.

Where we remain unconvinced is in the use of barbless hooks. It is our contention that if it is easier for us to unhook a pike with barbless hooks then it must be easier for the pike to do the same, especially if slack line is given, or if the pike head-thrashes on the surface. Advocates of barbless trebles have found to their bait-cost that one (bait-holding) point of the treble has to retain the barb to prevent the bait from falling off. That is precisely why we argue, and have proven to our satisfaction, that barbless hooks lose pike.

Many, sometimes extravagant, claims are made about the efficacy of single hooks, claims which we refute not so much because we doubt the percentage success rate but because we are satisfied that trebles are even more successful. If it concerns you that trebles may be swallowed and therefore difficult to remove, then factors outlined in paragraph two should be studied.

If, after all this discussion, you still prefer to use single hooks, then good patterns are available. Partridge manufacture perhaps the best purpose-designed pike single under the trade name of 'VB singles'. Only two sizes are available, Nos 6 and 8: strong, sharp, black hooks with straight eyes. At 180° to the shank is braised another single hook without an eye, Nos 8 and 10 respectively, which is the bait-holding hook. With the smaller hook inserted in the bait, the pike-hooking hook stands proud. We have a couple of comments to make about this particular design: (1) half of each packet of hooks should have a downturn eye so that when used in tandem the wire passing through the eye of the upper hook is not kinked, and (2) the bait-holding hook would be improved if it were the same size (or even one size larger) as the 'pike' hook. If these suggestions were to be put into practice, the single would offer improved bait-

holding capability when, for example, using the eye sockets of a deadbait to take the force of the cast. The No. 10, especially, is too narrow in gape to provide good purchase in, for instance, a large sardine or sizeable roach.

The second pattern of specially designed pike single, the 'Back-to-back' from Drennan, does offer such improved facility, but it could still be improved in the following ways. The hooks are short-shanked, offering a reduced braised area and, we feel, reduced strength. Simply by lengthening the shank these hooks would be made considerably stronger. Secondly, the large ring eye is in the same plane as the hooks—by turning it through 90° it could be better used as a 'keel' to hold the hook proud of the bait and it would probably improve hooking as a result.

The pike angler who prefers treble hooks (as do the authors) is much better served. Each of the major hook manufacturers offers a perfectly suitable pike treble which must be strong, sharp and small-barbed. Partridge 'outpoints' and 'Eagle Claw' are proven pike hooks (especially the latter) and, in general, we need look no further than these two patterns in Nos 8 and 10 for bait fishing. Additionally, the Partridge hooks offer a semi-barbless pattern in which two of the points are barbless, a small bait-holding barb being present on the third point.

Larger hook sizes, used with lures, are usually required to prevent the body of the lure actually masking the hook, and sizes 6 for some bar spoons (spinners) and 4 and 2 for spoons and plugs are generally the ones to aim for. Nearly all trebles of this size are sufficiently strong but a check should always be made, and one such that we use is to exert finger pressure on two prongs. If the tension prevents you from squeezing them together, the hook is plenty strong enough!

A versatile tandem-hook pike rig is made easily with the use of a 'Ryder' hook, which consists of a treble hook with an additional eye braised to the shank. The main eye of the hook is downturned, the wire being passed through this eye, once around the shank and through the small (extra) eye, and then along to the fixed bottom treble. In this way the 'Ryder' hook (see Fig. 1a) is moved easily along the wire to accommodate different bait sizes. Unfortunately, tradition has made the hook of square bend, and it is weaker as a result.

Fig. 1 shows the standard 'Snap Tackle', which is used almost exclusively by Barrie Rickards and consists of 18 inches of 18–20 lb b.s. wire, a Drennan swivel, No. 10 or 12, a size 8 'Ryder' hook (see Fig. 1a) and a size 8 or 10 'Eagle Claw' treble. Fig. 2 illustrates the rig baited with a 'half' mackerel, tail end. When using the head 'half' one point of the 'Ryder' hook is passed through both lips.

Fig. 3 shows the rig most commonly used by Martin Gay and comprises 18 inches of 20 lb PDQ stranded wire and the usual No. 10 and 12 Drennan Diamond eye swivel. A size 2 downturned eye single hook is fixed permanently in position by wrapping the wire 8–10 times around the shank (after first passing the wire through the eye). This single hook is used for bait holding (although it sometimes hooks the pike!) in the same way as the 'Ryder' hook, and is usually fixed 4 inches from a size 8 or 10 'Eagle Claw' treble. Several rigs need to be made up to accommodate various bait sizes. Fig. 4 shows the rig used on a sardine, with the single hook passing through the eye sockets. Figs 5–8 depict the range of trebles and singles described.

## Trace Roll

The trace roll in Fig. 9 is a Barrie Rickards' invention of many years' standing and is the ideal way of storing wire traces. Any suitable tin with a well-fitting lid, 6–8 inches long and 4 inches or so in diameter, can be used to hold the cork or polyethylene 'roll' around which are wrapped the traces. The bottom hook is nicked into the roll, and the trace swivel is held in place with a map pin. Since the trace is wrapped around a circumference of 9 inches, or thereabouts, it remains kink-free, is instantly available for use, and it does not become tangled.

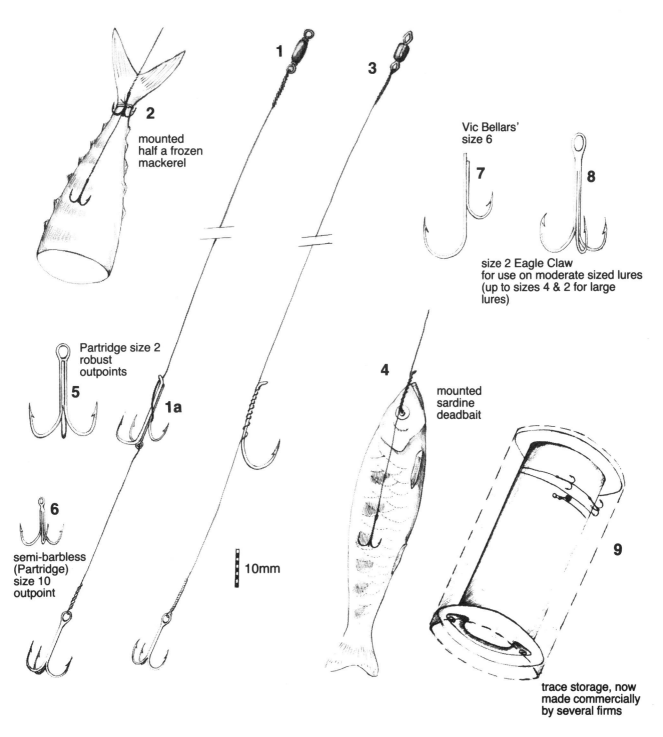

1

2 mounted half a frozen mackerel

3

Vic Bellars' size 6

7

8

size 2 Eagle Claw for use on moderate sized lures (up to sizes 4 & 2 for large lures)

Partridge size 2 robust outpoints

5

1a

4 mounted sardine deadbait

6

semi-barbless (Partridge) size 10 outpoint

10mm

9

trace storage, now made commercially by several firms

# LEADS

In pike fishing lead is rarely used to cock a float (the one notable exception is the vaned drifting float where it is most important), so the pike angler can immediately dispense with split shot from sizes 8 to AA, but 'swan' shot or SSG is used frequently. We usually use lead to hold a bait in position and/or to achieve distance casting with small baits. Arlesey Bombs or Pear leads from ½–3 oz cover most piking demands, although there are some exceptions.

Fig. 1 shows the standard Arlesey Bomb whose streamlined shape lends it to long casting. Whether the swivel actually performs a useful task is open to question, but a considerable saving in cost is achieved by using a pear lead, with no loss of distance. On large waters with strong undertow, and in rivers, even substantial Arlesey Bombs may be dragged from position by the current. Fig. 2 shows the same bomb after flattening with a hammer, which considerably improves 'bottom grip'.

As previously stated, Arlesey Bombs can prove expensive, and today not all tackle shops stock pear leads. In snag-ridden swims loss of expensive or hard-to-find tackle is clearly a disadvantage, so makeshift leads can be used. Fig. 3 shows one such weight that can be made very simply at home. It comprises a length of ½ inch O.D. copper tubing which is filled with molten lead (take care—wear goggles and handle the crucible with tongs), and has a wire ring or swivel (for the extravagant!) inserted in one end, to which the line is tied. By experiment various lengths of tube can then be cut to achieve a variety of weights. As a bonus they are also swan proof! Of course even home-made ledger weights are still lost in snags, but there are occasions when weight is needed only to aid casting, after which it is better dispensed with—such as when you want to free-line a small bait beyond its casting range. Cheap, even free (!), weights are needed here, where their loss does not matter. Fig. 4 details the most commonly used 'free' weight in the shape of a 'nut' which is tied to the link with PVA string. After 20–30 seconds (depending on water temperature) the PVA dissolves and the 'nut' falls away to leave a free-lined bait at whatever range you wish.

An alternative to both Figs 3 and 4, in that it is cheap and dispensable, is shown in Fig. 5, and consists of a (variable) length of cycle inner tube filled with sand, the two ends being closed with elastic bands or staples and one end being tied to a rotten bottom of 6 lb b.s. line. By varying the length of tube different weights can be made up. Barrie Rickards has used these 'leads' to good effect on the Relief Channel, much to the amusement of his friends. Probably because of their smooth outer surface these weights snag up less frequently than conventional leads, but at such a low cost it is of little consequence.

Quite often a small quantity of lead is needed, for example to keep a livebait at a fixed depth. Fig. 6 (barrel leads), Fig. 7 (drilled bullets) and Fig. 8 (swan shot) each achieve this and offer the necessary flexibility of weight through different sizes. Barrel leads and drilled bullets can be fished running on the line or fixed in position (by swan shot!), although if left free running they may come up against a knot and so we would recommend putting a bead between the lead and knot to prevent abrasion. The advantage of leads over swan shot is that they offer a concentrated weight in a small package and there is little risk of damaging the line, which is possible when pinching on split shot—see Fig. 8b.

The spiral lead, see Fig. 9, was popular 25 years ago with spinning enthusiasts when it was used to add or remove casting weight quickly to or from the line. The reel line was simply wound through the brass spiral at one end of the lead, continued around the grooved body and through the brass spiral at the opposite end. In this way it could be positioned anywhere along the line very promptly. However, it had two disadvantages: firstly, twisting the line around the brass spirals can kink the line (leading to a potential weak spot) and, secondly the lead can easily untwist itself from the line and depart! If you decide some weight is needed for a spinning or plugging trace, split shot or a barrel lead are just as efficient.

Continuing with our undesirable lead weights section, we come to Fig. 10, the 'Capta' lead. Relative newcomers to angling may not actually know this pattern, but it was quite popular in the mid 1960s and was offered as a ledger weight for running water. The theory was that the three converging flat surfaces pushed by the current kept the lead on the bottom. A flattened Arlesey Bomb is every bit as efficient in practice *and* it casts well. The Capta lead gives poor casting distance, is inaccurate and, even more infuriating, it 'planes' under water so that the bait actually ends up in a completely different area from that intended. 'Capta' leads have no place in pike angling!

Slightly more accurate in casting, but offering little other advantage, is the 'Coffin' lead shown in Fig. 11. At a pinch it could replace a barrel lead or drilled bullet, and its flattened cross-section may be of some use to hold position in a current. It is a design prone to snagging.

Holding the bait in one spot in a strong current is a problem, and depends on more than just weight and design. We detail the correct technique on page 34, but matters can most certainly be improved with the use of the lead shown in Fig. 12. It may be a strange contraption, but it works on the same principle as a ship's anchor chain; i.e., the anchor itself does not hold an ocean liner in place, rather the length of chain let out does. Weigh out more chain until a position is held. In Fig. 12 are two fixed leads set 12–14 in. apart, the left-hand lead being the heavier of the two. In practice a better hold on the river bed is achieved with, say, a combined weight of 1¼ oz (¾ oz for the intermediate lead, ½ oz for the terminal lead) than with a single 1½ or even 2 oz lead. It is less drag for a running fish and is cheaper in the event of a loss!

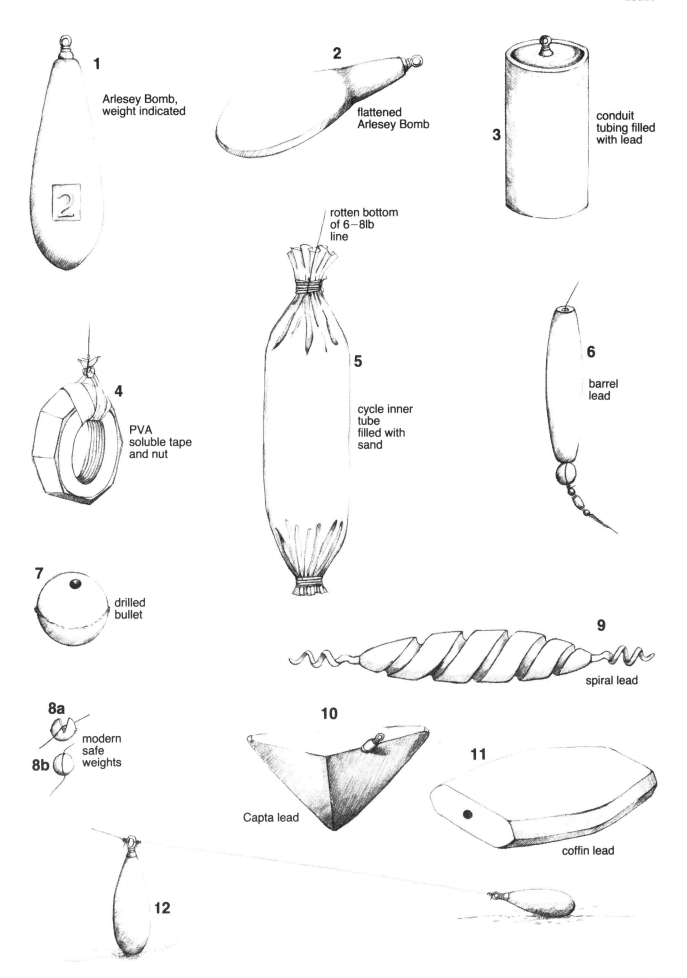

1 Arlesey Bomb, weight indicated

2 flattened Arlesey Bomb

3 conduit tubing filled with lead

4 PVA soluble tape and nut

5 rotten bottom of 6–8lb line

cycle inner tube filled with sand

6 barrel lead

7 drilled bullet

8a modern safe weights
8b

9 spiral lead

10 Capta lead

11 coffin lead

12

# BITE INDICATORS

Positive bite, or more correctly 'run' indication, is singularly the most important aid to pike conservation in practical angling terms, and it is to this end that we cannot over-emphasise the need to remain alert to any signal which may mean that a pike is in the vicinity of, or has actually taken, the bait.

Early and *reliable* indication of a 'take', coupled with bait size, hook arrangements and any previous knowledge of feeding habits are of special importance to prevent deep hooking. The aim, always, is to hook the pike in the jaws or forward part of the mouth, the strike being made as soon as you are reasonably sure that the hooks are inside the mouth. With this in mind we use a number of indicator methods, some of which may seem to involve a 'belt-and-braces' approach, relying as we do on up to three separate, though supporting, indicators at the same time. In this way, should one system fail another will signal the run. In heavy water, either a strong current or big wave/undertow conditions, it is not difficult for a run to go undetected if, to give as an example, the tow has previously submerged the float. But with the addition of a bobbin-style indicator and line clip any run towards or away from the rod will show.

A study of figures 1–5 gives the detail of some of the run indication methods we prefer; all are positioned at the reel end of the tackle and each can be used with or without a float—usually, we might add, *with* the float. We have our own particular favourites, Figs 2 and 5 for Barrie, Figs 1 and 3 for Martin, although Barrie is quickly being converted to Fig. 1!

As a generalisation 'drop-back' takes are not a regular feature of the authors' fishing, because we often use a float and are not afraid to put on a fair amount of lead if necessary. However, sunken float techniques, and fishing in fog, always impress upon us the need to cover all eventualities and are one of the reasons why the method described first, and shown as Fig. 1, is gaining in popularity.

*Fig. 1 (and 1a)* This simple and thoroughly reliable system has the double advantage of showing runs away from the rod *and* slack line takes. The line is fished under tension between the float and/or lead and bait, and is clipped immediately above the reel spool to the rod handle with a John Roberts' line clip. The bobbin, fished tight up to the rod, is plastic, has a 1-inch diameter and is 1–2 inches long. It needs to be of sufficient weight to drop against the tension of the line in the event of a pike running towards the rod. The bobbin is not left permanently on the line but is cut along its length for speedy addition or removal, and we recommend it is removed before striking. If a float is also used, the tension on the line sometimes partly submerges it but often, as the pike takes the bait and momentarily slackens the line, the float pops up to the surface. This slight slackening of the line usually causes the bobbin to drop fractionally—a full-blooded run pulls the line clear of the clip and trots

away unhindered. The sharp dotted line in the figure shows the position of the bobbin with a slack line bite, and the curved dashed line indicates the action of the line with a run.

For unusually thick rod handles which will not take J.R. run clips a strip of plastic can be taped to the rod (directly above the usual reel position) to produce the same effect. Clip the line only enough to grip it lightly: too much tension can cause the odd dropped run. The only other disadvantage we have found is that very, very occasionally the bobbin may spin after a rapid take, twisting the line and perhaps jamming in the rod ring. In practice this has happened only twice to date, but it should be borne in mind.

We have included in Fig. 1 the use of an Optonic alarm, partly for reasons of completeness but also because we are using audible alarms rather more regularly these days.

*Fig. 2* Barrie has used what he calls 'the silver paper method' for a great many years and it has therefore served the test of time. The line is held against the rod handle by a fold of aluminium foil and its advantages include high visibility and noise on release. By tighter pinching of the foil it will overcome quite considerable line drag, but because the foil remains 'soft' it does not appear to cause dropped runs. It cannot, of course, detect drop-back bites, so this method must be used with a float or tight, observable line. Various thicknesses of foil can be used to combat conditions on the day, but it is important to smooth all outside edges as the risk is for the foil cylinder to snag on the line. When a run occurs the foil falls clear of the line, giving the pike unhindered line from the spool.

*Fig. 3* This has been a firm favourite of ours for many years and only recently has it given way to the system described in Fig. 1. The biggest single advantage when using the empty spool indicator is that once the pike has pulled the line clear it is completely free to run off. The disadvantages are much like those for Fig. 2 in that it alone cannot signal a slack line take. Undertow or current may be overcome by either pushing the spool further into the ground or, preferably, by loading it with gravel. There is little disadvantage in this so long as you use only sufficient additional weight to overcome the line drag. It is a simple and effective system, but we recommend its use only in conjunction with a float. Other drawbacks? It is possible that a loop of line might catch around the reel after a take, if the run pauses after jerking away from the spool; once Barrie had a run so fast that it rammed the spool onto the rod blank! Clearly, with modern carbon fibre rods this might just prove expensive, especially if the empty spool has previously been loaded with gravel!

*Fig. 4* The 'drop-arm' system has gained a considerable following through recent seasons, being consistently reliable, and highly visible and audible when connected to a mercury tilt switch or similar elec-

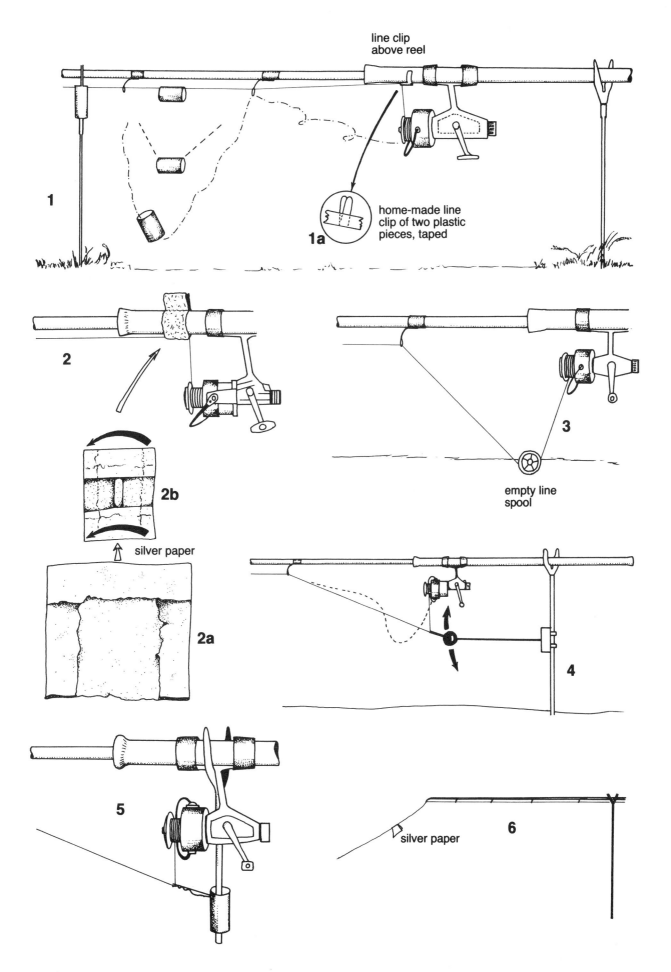

line clip
above reel

home-made line
clip of two plastic
pieces, taped

**1**

**1a**

**2**

**2b**

silver paper

**2a**

**3**

empty line
spool

**4**

**5**

silver paper **6**

tronic alarm. The line is held under tension through a diamond clip—from which it can easily be detached—which in turn is attached to a 1–1½ inch table tennis ball painted day-glo orange. This sight ball is at the end of an 8–10 inch arm which is clipped to the rear rod rest; the arm must be of metal rod if connected to an electronic arm but in a passive system can be of cord. With the rod in two rests the reel is positioned directly above the sight ball. A run away from the rod pulls the line free of the clip, the ball then falling to the ground, or if connected electronically to an alarm it drops to activate the buzzer. An electronic system should be chosen with care as some switches are insufficiently sensitive to set off an alarm with only a slight slackening of the line. We can recommend the Eddie Turner drop-back alarm for reliability and sensitivity, although even with this design we have known the arm to freeze in the horizontal position. Obviously it is not a problem if you choose a passive system whereby the sight ball is attached to the rod rest with a cord.

The line must be fished under tension for the system to indicate a slack line take, and really the only risk as we see it is the faint chance of a coil of line snagging at the reel, as in Fig. 3.

Fig. 5 We first saw this system in use in 1970 on the London reservoirs—rather like a Heath Robinson sort of design—and it has recently become a firm favourite with Barrie, particularly when ledgering. A hair grip is pushed through the side of a cylinder of plastic 2–3 inches long and 1 inch in diameter, which is then slid along the rear rod rest so that it can rise and fall freely. The reel is positioned directly above the rear rod rest, as in the diagram, the line again being fished under some tension (although this is not critical, it is preferable). Painting the cylinder day-glo orange produces a highly visible bite indicator. On a concrete or hard gravel bank a degree of audible indication is also achieved: the line pulls free of the hair grip and as the indicator chatters down the metal rod rest it 'clunks' as it hits the ground. It is particularly wind-resistant and, by pushing the line into one of three notches in the hair grip, it is resistant to quite considerable line drag.

At present it cannot adequately detect slack line takes, and that flying loop of line, again, might just catch the reel. This latter possibility is one that is always present with any rear-rod-rest attached system, but in practice it very rarely is a problem; however, it is as well to be aware of the danger—trapped line can cause a dropped bait and at worst can result in the loss of the rod as everything is pulled in!

A number of other bite indication systems are in common use with pike anglers, the methods so far described we know, use and trust. Some pikers use the 'carp' anglers' popular 'monkey-climber' system but to us it seems unnecessary, and it is worth mentioning that it is a method which actually increases resistance to the run as the bobbin rises along the stick. We will have more to say about resistance elsewhere, but for the present we will detail just one more indicator, especially popular, it seems, amongst Fenland pike fishermen.

Fig. 6 When fishing a drain or other water with steep banks it is sometimes necessary to space the rods to one side of the sitting position, looking along the bank for indications of a run. If, to complicate matters further, vegetation is particularly high, all that is sometimes visible is the top section of the rod. Butt indicators, unless audible, are hidden from view and are therefore useless. One way around this is achieved by pinching a 'flag' of aluminium foil to the line immediately beyond the rod tip. By tightening up to the bait and then clipping the line at the reel, you have an efficient and very visual indicator for both slack line and tight line runs. However, if the margins are too deep to wade to the rod end it can be awkward attaching the flag, in which case it is better to place a 'bobbin' between the furthest two rings that you can reach. Also, if the foil snags the line or jams in the top ring, retrieving the tackle or a fish can be perilous.

For these latter reasons we do not use this method, preferring the bobbin-between-the-furthest-rings approach, but with care it is another system to use in particular circumstances.

It should be noted that all pike run indicators are usually used with an open pick-up, allowing free line to a running fish. One final note: the float is the very best run indicator we know and we use one whenever the technique permits, many times in conjunction with one of the systems described in Figs 1–5. The very best indicators are superfluous if, having signalled a run, you delay the strike for the next ten minutes. Knowing the correct time to strike, of course, comes with experience and can vary from water to water, and day to day, but as a generalisation the 'best' time is when the run is doing something positive. This can mean running steadily or not running at all. Twitchy, jerky takes often signal small fish, but if the twitching continues for more than 15–20 seconds the strike should be made because if it happens to be a big fish the bait is probably being swallowed on the spot.

*Pike conservation starts, and finishes, with good bite indication.*

# FLOATS

Floats have two uses in pike angling, and also additional benefits in particular circumstances. Primarily, they are superb run indicators, probably the very best, by being 'close' to the bait. All takes, no matter what form, show first on the float. On waters where pike habitually swallow the bait on the spot, *if given the chance*, a sensitively arranged float is a must to prevent deep hooking. The second use of the float, and often of equal importance, is to enable the bait to be fished in a certain manner. Drifting and fishing a chosen depth are two of the most obvious examples.

All our floats are fished as sliders, with either a central hole or ring fixed to the bottom, and are stopped at the required depth with the usual stop-knot-and-bead arrangement. The bead can be either a commercially purpose-made one, such as the John Roberts' black bead which is 5 mm in diameter (the hole is actually larger than it needs to be), or one simply taken from a cheap imitation-pearl necklace. Stop knots, which must slide easily but not continuously, are made from monofilament nylon or heavy gauge whipping thread, either as a series of granny knots or the proper 'Billy Lane' sliding knot. Care must be taken not to overtighten the knot for fear of weakening the line.

When fishing a deadbait on the bottom, and occasionally a ledgered livebait, we usually set the float to fish over-depth, sometimes by as much as 50% depending on the water conditions: the greater the over-depth setting, the more likely the float will remain on the surface in a current, even though the line is tensioned by the same current. The float is cocked with a combination of the 'weight' of the terminal tackle and the tension on the line between the float and the reel. All our surface-fished floats are painted to have a dark coloured underside and a day-glo orange or pink top. (Floats used for sunken float paternostering, etc. naturally are painted matt green, brown or black.) When cocked the float shows the day-glo colour. However, because the float is not self-cocking, as soon as the bait is picked up and the tension is released the weight of the line between the float and the rod tips the float over to show the dark underside. This is the very earliest run indication, although we should say that on many occasions the float merely disappears or runs away across the surface. When fishing with an oily deadbait, such as a mackerel, and sometimes herring, sardine or trout, an oil-slick may appear immediately down-wind of the float (see Fig. 1; the arrow indicates wind direction) at about the same time as the float tips over. In very windy conditions, or whenever the float has been taken under by the drift or current, this oil slick indicates a 'take' before any other method. The quantity of oil released from the deadbait depends on the bait type and freshness, and the amount of chewing the pike gives the bait.

The bait being picked up releases some of the tension on the line, which is usually indicated at the rod. If a bobbin is attached to the line, there is often a slight slackening of position.

Fig. 2 details the authors' preferred 'standard' float rig. Distance *a* is the depth set between the stop knot and the trace swivel, distance *b* varies from zero (for deadbaiting) to perhaps 2 feet (for paternostered livebait). To enable the float to surface quickly, even on heavy breaking strain line, it can have quite a large bore (up to only slightly less than the diameter of the bead). The swan shot, or ledger stop, is used to prevent the float from sliding down over the trace. The distance between the stop and the trace must be greater than the length of the trace to prevent the livebait from swimming up and hooking over the stop. Apart from fishing badly, it would result in a 'bite off' as soon as the pike took the bait, the line passing across its teeth. With a very narrow diameter bore through the float it is quite feasible to leave off the stop, allowing the float to rest against the trace swivel before the cast, especially when bottom fishing a deadbait. With a paternostered livebait it may, however, increase the risk of a tangle during the cast, in which case it is better to separate the float and the trace with the stop.

Figs 3 and 4 detail a drifting float which is the result of many hours' field-testing by its designers, Colin Dyson and Archie Braddock. The float comprises a balsa body, 8 inches long, into which is inserted and glued a $2\frac{1}{2} \times \frac{1}{4}$ inch dowel stem. This stem is wrapped with sufficient lead wire to cock the float to approximately $\frac{1}{4}$ inch below a sliding ring inserted in the side of the float. A second ring is whipped to the bottom of the dowel stem. The positioning of the top sliding ring and the amount of lead wire needed are critical, and tests should be conducted in a bucket of water before each is permanently fixed. It is important that the ring remains above the water line to keep all of the line on the surface. The vane, $2\frac{1}{4}$ inches square, is inserted and glued into the top of the balsa body and is entirely responsible for the drifting capacity of the float. Stiff, but flexible plastic, such as that used in some yoghurt containers or microwave oven utensils, is the finest material for the vane and it does not in practice appear to matter whether the vane is flat or curved.

The float is again fished as a slider, the line being greased under most situations, although in a cross-wind a better drift is sometimes achieved with an ungreased line.

The float is self-cocking, but it is important to add some lead above the trace—swan shot or a barrel lead—to keep the bait near the required depth. This additional lead/bait may affect the position at which the float cocks and rides the surface and subsequent adjustment to the lead wire may be necessary while fishing initially.

The vane and top inch of the balsa body are painted

day-glo orange or pink, which is highly visible at a distance of 200 yards or more. We especially like this design of drifting float which carries the bait away at a sensible and leisurely pace. We want all the water to be covered with equal effectiveness throughout the drift, and the use of an over-large fixed vane sometimes takes the bait through an area rather too quickly. You can, of course, check the line at any point during the drift in order to hold the bait in one position for longer. However, this will usually result in the float moving off to one side, depending on the strength and direction of the wind, but in so doing it covers extra water before the drift away is allowed to commence.

There are, it must be said, a number of designs for drifting floats, some incorporating dart flights and others with two offset vanes, and in practice they rate from useless to satisfactory. Fig. 5 illustrates a second pattern which we like especially for its simplicity. Hertfordshire anglers Eddie Turner and Vic Gibson are responsible for the design, again the result of many hours of field testing and modification. It consists of a 13-inch silver steel stem, with an eye at each end through which the reel line runs freely, a plastic vane, $4 \times 3\frac{1}{2}$ inches, attached to the stem by an elastic band and a $1\frac{1}{2}$-inch polystyrene ball body to give the required buoyancy. The 'ET' float, as it is now known and marketed, has certain advantages over other designs, especially its visibility. The vanes are interchangeable, offering greater drifting potential: in light winds a larger vane can be added; in strong winds the rate of drift can be varied by using larger or smaller vanes. Furthermore, large baits can be carried by adding a second polyball to the stem to increase buoyancy without affecting its drifting speed.

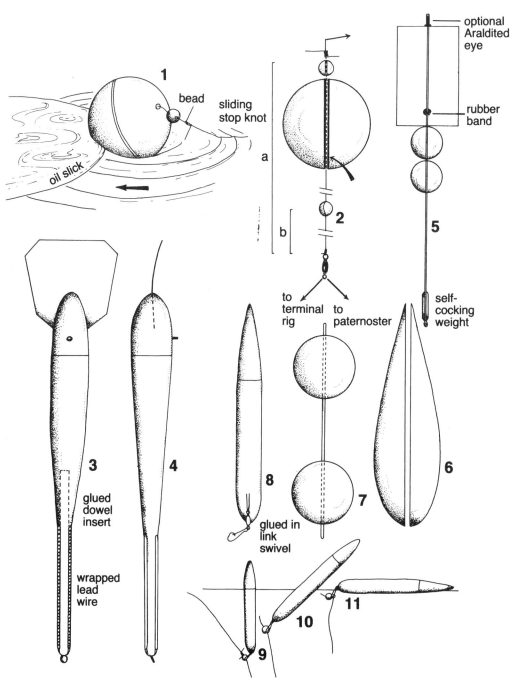

The 'ET' float as described is commercially available. The top eye is detachable from the stem, in the belief that it will aid striking at long range by reducing the drag—the top eye comes away as you tighten up firmly so that the strike is made through the (fixed) bottom eye. We question the need for this: firstly, because we have not found the drag an impediment on the strike and, secondly, if the eye pulls off the stem, it is possible for the vane to come adrift of the stem and sink! If you wish to drift with the float attached through the bottom eye, there is no need to remove the top eye, merely thread the line only through the bottom eye! We glue the detachable top eye permanently in position.

The only other comment to make is that we believe the design is improved by glueing a small barrel lead along the bottom of the stem to render the float self-cocking. Without this, and when using small baits and little lead at the trace, the wind can blow the float flat!

These two factors apart, the 'ET' float works well, although in use it is really no better (or worse) than the Dyson/Braddock design (Figs 3 and 4). Both floats will take 4–6 oz baits to the limit of the reel's line capacity.

The very best drifting wind is one which blows directly away from the fishing bank. With a greased line the wind acting on the vane will take line unaided for quite a distance until (assuming the use of a fixed spool reel) the line has a considerable lip to climb from the spool. After this it is necessary to pay out line manually unless you choose a very free-running centre pin or multiplier reel. At present we prefer the fixed spool reel and manual line pay-out, although there is a gadget called 'an automatic drifting pin' which is the height of laziness!

Winds blowing diagonally off the fishing bank also provide excellent drifting conditions when an enormous volume of water can be covered. It may, in particular circumstances, be advantageous to use ungreased line in these conditions, as the line bow formed in the wind can actually drag the float back to the bank. In relatively calm conditions it is usually necessary to cast 20–30 yards initially to get the float out beyond the wind 'shadow' and also to give plenty of free line until the float 'bites' in the wind. Obviously larger vanes help.

Figs 6 and 8–11 show streamline floats where, correctly, the *fat* end of the float casts into the wind and thereafter remains downwards in the water. When chasing maximum casting distance and minimum resistance to a running fish the float in Fig. 6 is probably the ideal shape. Streamlining floats is also assisted by the use of a smooth and glossy exterior finish. Figs 3, 4 and 5 are not streamline designs because exactly the opposite effect is desired—maximum resistance to the air/water is needed in order to achieve slow, deliberate drifting over a considerable distance.

The famous Dennis Pye dumb-bell float is detailed in Fig. 7 and comprises two spheres, each 1½–2 inches in diameter, connected by a dowel peg. The float is fished as a slider (two rings, one whipped to each sphere), but the reasoning behind its design has always puzzled us. Two spheres, each with a diameter of 2 inches, have a total surface area of 25 square inches and a total volume of 8.37 cubic inches, which in the water create as much drag and resistance as a single sphere with a diameter of almost 3 inches. No sensible pike angler would dream of using such a float under all usual circumstances, so we deduce from this that the dumb-bell float has not been used for its *lack* of resistance, but rather because of the extra resistance it offers the wind to assist drift. A bait would have much difficulty pulling such a float, which perhaps explains why Dennis Pye used large livebaits. Putting two half-inch diameter floats on one peg, he could have used 4 oz livebaits and achieved just as much drift and 'searchability'.

Fig. 8 is the more or less standard 'cigar float'. We make ours from a half-inch diameter balsa rod about 6 inches in length, although of course this length is highly variable. We especially like these floats because they are particularly visible, with up to 2 inches showing above the water; they offer little resistance; and they show so much more about what the livebait is doing. For example, it is often possible to tell if the bait, especially rudd, has tangled with the reel line, since in so doing it usually takes a little of the tension from the lead, lifting the float slightly and holding it higher in the water. Very many pike takes lift the bait and lead from their fixed position (float paternostering) before running away, so you get a particularly early indication as the float lifts and keels over lift-method fashion. This slim, low resistance float is, however, easily submerged in a heavy **chop** or current, but it is possible to overcome **much** of the problem by using increasingly longer floats—although there comes a point after which you might as well use a sturdier design, such as a 1½ inch diameter polystyrene ball. We fish this float bottom end, as a slider, the line running through a swivel eye glued into the base. The clip link is an optional extra facilitating speedy float changing.

Figs 9–11 show the float in action. In Fig. 9 the float is exactly at depth, while in Fig. 10 it is only slightly over depth, or lifted due to bait activity, or lifted momentarily after a pike strike. In Fig. 11 the float is set too much over-depth, but if the float suddenly changes position from Figs 9 to 11 it is almost certainly a take. For close range fishing with 1–3 oz baits in calm conditions, when it is possible to use small paternoster leads, we like this float for it adds a certain refinement to the tackle. However, it is not a fetish and we must emphasise that a float is there to be seen, to indicate a take immediately it occurs. Sunken float techniques, which we think *have* become a fetish with some people, are an important additional technique to be used in special circumstances only.

# RIGS (1) LEDGERING

With the present accent on drifting methods and long range casting, on big pits, broads and reservoirs, two or three 'delicate' piking techniques have rather been forgotten. One such is the free-lined livebait, a technique which was very much in vogue in the early 1970s. Obviously its limitations centre around the distance such a bait can be cast (although a bait could be 'ballooned' out, serious bite detection problems would result), but on small waters, or drains where pike are habitually close in, the method is particularly successful and is especially so on waters where the pike are under heavy angling pressure.

The tackle in Fig. 1 is fished totally free of weight except, of course, for the trace. The bait, usually liphooked, is lowered or cast gently into position and is usually allowed to swim to the bottom. By keeping the line under the merest tension it can be felt when the bait has reached its resting place, at which point the slack line is taken up *gently* and a sensitive bite indicator is fixed in position. Slack line bites are common on free-lined tackle, as are gentle pick-ups, so a careful watch should be kept at all times on the line/indicator.

If the current or undertow is too strong or extra casting range is required, a ledger weight can be added—fixed or sliding—above the trace and stopped before the swivel either with a bead (internal bore diameter *must* slide over the knot) or swan shot. Fig. 2 shows the standard arrangement for all river fishing and still water fishing with small baits and/or long range. If a tandem hook rig is preferred, one hook is passed through both lips, the bottom hook between the pelvic fins. If distance is not important, it is quite permissible to rig the bait up in the usual fashion, with the top hook in the base of the dorsal fin and the bottom hook in the pectoral muscle or top lip. Contrary to popular belief this does not pull the bait on its side, and even in situations where it may occur this does not detract from its pike-catching capacity.

When ledgering a live or deadbait at long range and/or in deep water, the trace sometimes folds back, the hooks tangle with the reel line (see Fig. 9) and a bite-off results. Fig. 2a details the rig which avoids this. Quite simply, about 12 inches of 20 lb b.s. line is tied to the trace. A second swivel is tied to the other end of this, which in turn is tied to the reel line. The top (second) swivel acts as the ledger stop.

It is worth knowing that a second benefit of freezing deadbaits (the first benefit being casting) is to cause the bait to sink slowly while still frozen, or, if a lead is used, to rise a little distance off the bottom and then to sink very slowly as the bait thaws. When fishing over silkweed or silt this allows the bait to rest on top of the weed rather than being dragged into it. Fig. 3 shows the effect.

Frozen smelt, for some reason, take much longer to thaw out than other deadbaits and in cold water may take 30 minutes to soften. Additionally, this seems to cause rather more dropped runs, and perhaps we should add that it is also necessary to use a lead with frozen smelt (see Fig. 4) if you wish to keep them close to the bottom.

If, however, you want the deadbait to stay permanently off the bottom (perhaps to fish it clear of rooted weed), you can achieve this in one of two ways. The first of these is to use natural freshwater baits, leaving the swim-bladder intact; the second, and one which can be used with fresh or salt water baits, is to inject the bait by syringe with sufficient air to cause it to float. Some fish, sardines for example, will not hold air; roach and rudd, on the other hand, hold air very well. To tether the bait in position, lead (which can be fixed if preferred) is again added up-trace, and if running lead is used line can be fed to the bait (see Fig. 5) to float it up to any chosen depth. The bait can be floated right up to the surface, of course, where it can be twitched over weedbeds, etc. This is not an especially good technique, but it is worth bearing in mind.

A bait which will not hold injected air can be made buoyant by inserting a polystyrene or balsa wood rod into the fish's throat. Fig. 6 shows the method using a whole bait.

Fig. 7 shows a head (mackerel) ready for casting. Two-hook rigs really must be used on baits of this size. The sliding, or top (if fixed), hook must be passed through both lips, or eye sockets if a small bait is used, for trouble-free long casting. The bottom hook is positioned in what would be the shoulder of the fish and near to the top of the flank.

Head 'half' baits cast true and generally further than tail ends. Frozen tail half baits, unless absolutely flat, often spiral in flight, which reduces distance. The common cause of this is the tail fin and trimming the fin back to the tail root (Fig. 8) effectively deals with the problem. If absolute distance is necessary, streamlining the bait (shown by the broken line) may achieve a little more distance.

Fig. 9: as previously mentioned when describing Fig. 2a, baits sometimes twist back along the line during the cast. There are two further effective rigs which can eliminate this. The first is to fish the bait paternoster style, particularly with small baits, where the lead link is longer than the trace (in Fig. 10 Y is greater than X). By placing a fixed tube on the lead link at the required position the bait can be tied with PVA string to hold it firmly in place during the cast. That is the second anti-backlash approach, although you may find when using large (4 oz or more) baits that it is better to tie the bait to the lead rather than to the link. This concentration of weight will actually cast better.

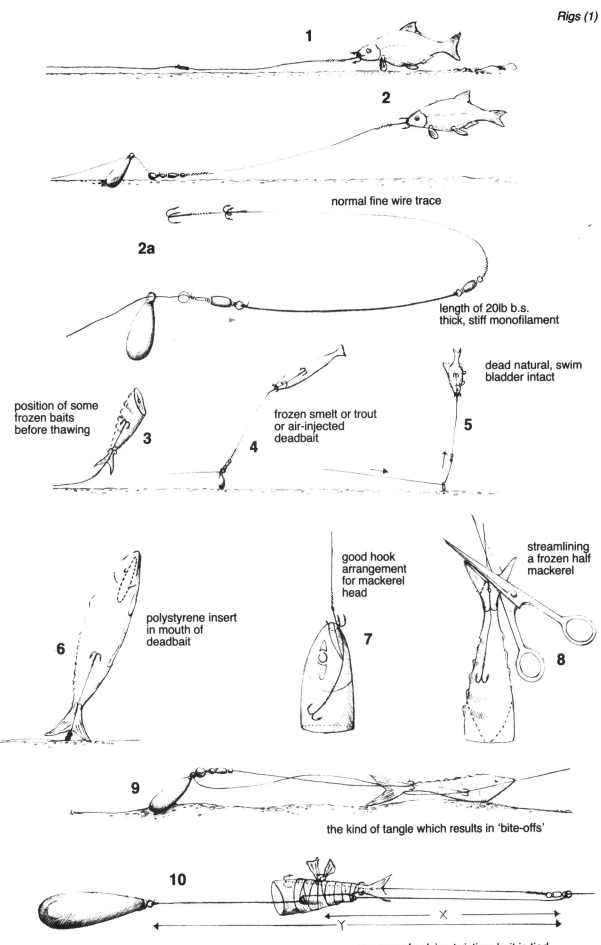

**1**

**2**

normal fine wire trace

**2a**

length of 20lb b.s.
thick, stiff monofilament

position of some
frozen baits
before thawing

**3**

frozen smelt or trout
or air-injected
deadbait

**4**

dead natural, swim
bladder intact

**5**

polystyrene insert
in mouth of
deadbait

**6**

good hook
arrangement
for mackerel
head

**7**

streamlining
a frozen half
mackerel

**8**

**9**

the kind of tangle which results in 'bite-offs'

**10**

X

Y

one way of solving twisting: bait is tied
to tube or swivels with PVA tape
(for heavy baits X should equal Y)

# RIGS (2) PATERNOSTERS

There is really little doubt that the paternoster method of presenting live and deadbaits is the most productive pike-taking technique. It also causes many people a lot of trouble!

Fig. 1 shows the standard float paternoster set-up. The sliding float is stopped at the required depth (usually at the surface!) by the time-honoured bead-and-stop knot arrangement. To prevent the float from sliding down and over the trace swivel a split shot, or 'John Roberts ledger stop', is placed on the line 15–18 inches up from the trace. However, with the now common use of polystyrene balls for pike floats, such tiny diameter holes can be drilled through the ball that this 'stop' can be omitted. (There is a second bonus which we shall discuss in relation to Fig. 4.) The reel line is tied to the trace swivel and the paternoster link, usually of weaker line (6 lb), is tied to the bottom eye of this same swivel. The lead is attached to the link. The length of this lead link depends entirely on the depth the bait is to be fished off the bottom and how much freedom of movement the bait is intended to have. We tend to fish the set-up a little over-depth and with a long lead link-up of 3 or 4 feet to give the livebait plenty of freedom (see Fig. 3).

The weight of lead used is governed by the bait size and strength, casting distance and current. It is worth noting that with resistance-shy pike, i.e. those subject to heavy angling pressure, the lightest lead commensurate with other considerations should be used. The float paternoster rig is usually fished with the float on the surface. If wind-caused undertow, or current, is excessive, if boats also use the water, or if fishing is at such a range or in such conditions that the float is dragged under or cannot be seen, then setting the stop knot shallower than the depth of water immediately converts the arrangement to sunk-float paternoster. We must point out, however, that an additional bite indicator method will then be required. Figs 2a and 2b show the two arrangements.

Some anglers have difficulties with paternoster tackle and these usually centre around tangles with livebaits. Because the bait is tethered, it only has limited movement up and down, although it can describe a full circle, and this is the root cause of the problem. The bait, swimming in a circular manner, builds up a twist in the line which can sometimes spiral the reel line until it drags the float under. This causes the reel line to come into contact with the trace, which may result in a 'bite off'. And if that is not enough, the bait can also swim up, tangling the hooks with the reel line and producing the same result! This is further aggrevated if the distance between the stop-shot and the trace swivel is less than the length of the trace. If it is, the bait can actually hang up on the split-shot. In Fig. 4 distance X must be greater than distance Y unless, as previously mentioned, floats with a tiny internal bore are used, in which case distance X does not exist and the problem does not occur.

However, tangles are not all tactical. Some baits are definitely more tangle-inducing—rudd, perhaps, being the worst, as they naturally try to swim upwards. A hook placed in the dorsal area throws the bait off-balance, which further increases the chance of a tangle as it swims spiral-fashion towards the surface. The simplest and actually most effective way to prevent tangles is to liphook the bait: the difference is then quite dramatic.

A further refinement in our efforts to solve paternoster tangles can be seen in Fig. 5, and consists of a 2-inch length of black plastic tube which is fitted over the lead-link and held in place against the trace swivel with a split shot. The tube keeps the trace and the lead-link separated, but will not stop the bait from tangling the reel line. It is, in essence, a casting anti-tangle rig.

One of several seemingly doubtful piking techniques that we use is the paternostered deadbait, even half bait. Fig. 6 shows the arrangement with the bait in position, the only difference being that the stop shot can be positioned against the trace as there is no fear of the bait swimming upwards (or downwards for that matter!)

Primarily, the paternoster arrangement is used to hold the bait in one position and at approximately the same depth. The float is necessary to hold the bait up, the lead to keep it down. Where possible the float is used as the primary bite indicator, but it is also a very effective method of keeping the line between the float and the rod near to the surface and above any snags. Where snags are a potential hazard, and may foul the lead link when a fish is running with the bait, the smallest lead possible should be used on a 'rotten bottom'. For longer casting with heavier leads, perhaps up to 2 oz, the link will have to be of the same breaking strain as the reel line. This does not appear to deter the pike in most instances.

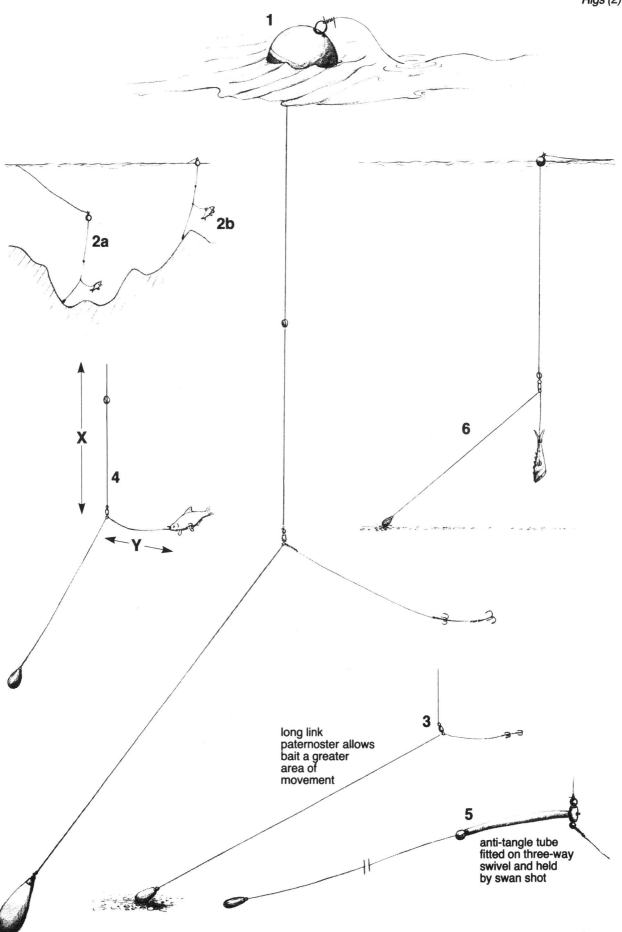

long link
paternoster allows
bait a greater
area of
movement

anti-tangle tube
fitted on three-way
swivel and held
by swan shot

# RIGS (3) VARIOUS

There is a school of thought—to which we do not belong—which argues that to hook pike successfully the hook(s) must first be pulled out of the bait before finding a hold in the pike's jaw. The debate further implies that with the pike firmly clamped on the bait it is impossible to move the bait, and hooks, on the strike and thereby to set the hooks. There are several loopholes in this claim and they can be set out as follows. We have caught considerable numbers of pike with the deadbait still attached to the hooks, and indeed we often tie the baits to the hooks and trace with 6 lb b.s. nylon line to ensure that they stay on them. With small baits, sprats and the like, the bait is often engulfed and once inside the mouth the jaws are not clamped on it, assuming that it even matters if they are. Thirdly, the advocates of this general argument ignore the supposed problem when they use livebaits!

In the early 1970s Alan Beat, who is both a follower of this reasoning as well as a champion of single hooks for pike, devised an ingenious rig incorporating both aspects. Fig. 1a details the arrangement. It is claimed by a number of users to be an instant strike rig; however, it is not, at least no more so than any rig incorporating twin hooks. To enable the hooks to be pulled free of the bait on the strike (or to enable the bait to fall free of the hooks during the fight!) the hooks are only lightly nicked into the skin of the deadbait, but this will not allow forceful casting. So, Alan devised an arrangement which took all the force of the cast without pulling on the hooks. It is achieved as follows: a loop of nylon is either tied to the root of the tail or, in the case of soft baits or those species without a noticeable 'wrist', threaded through the tail root; a second loop of nylon is then tied to the trace swivel. These two loops are tied together with PVA tape, or string, and this alone takes all the force of the cast. The total length of the double loop is only 3–5 inches, which allows the trace and hooks to be baited up without tension and without the hooks (lightly hooked) tearing out of the bait. Shortly after the cast the PVA dissolves, leaving the reel line straight through to the trace in the normal way. Partridge 'VB' hooks (see Fig. 1b) can be used, although Alan himself uses sizes 4 and 2 singles lightly nicked under the skin. Softer skinned baits, like herrings and sardines, are clearly better than mackerel or perch, which in the latter case would best be rigged with 'VB' hooks.

We believe that treble hooks are perfectly satisfactory, but we will concede that there is little to choose between a large single (No. 4 or 2) and a small treble (8 or 10) when using sprat-size baits. In fact, a perfectly good single hook rig can be used on such deadbaits, as in Fig. 2. The hook must be large—size 2—and should be hooked under the back-bone at the point of balance if the deadbait is to hang on an even keel. Small hooks are masked by the bait: the gape has to be wider than the width of the bait's back. The bait often comes back with the pike for use a second time, if it has not been badly cut up.

Deadbait wobbling has its advocates, John Sidley being one such successful angler, and indeed in the mid-1960s many active pike anglers did little else! A number of rigs were invented at the time, and many problems resulted which centred around poor hooking and the bait tearing after repeated casting. In Fig. 3 we show a very simple but good wobbling rig, which is simply the same tackle that Martin Gay uses for nearly all of his deadbaiting. The large single is hooked through both eye sockets, the skull then takes the force of the cast. The treble, size 8, or even 6, is hooked in the back, flank or between the pelvic fins depending on personal preference. In the latter position the treble has a 'keel' effect which may be useful. Hooked in the flank, the bait can be bent slightly to give it an eccentric retrieve, but this is not at all life-like and is probably no improvement on the standard fit-and-start retrieve.

Certain softer skinned baits split after several casts; it is caused by the bait's impact with the water. The problem can be almost eliminated, as Jim Gibbinson discovered many years ago, by slitting the abdomen and removing the innards. Perfectionists can re-stitch the cut but little benefit is derived from doing so.

Few modern pike anglers will have firsthand experience of the Archer Flight (Fig. 4), although it is still available through specialist catalogues and tackle shops. The Archer Flight is designed to spin a deadbait on a central axis, a technique which is rarely used today. The needle is pushed down the bait's throat and the hinged spinning flight is then closed around the head for additional purchase. Tandem traces position hooks along each flank, two trebles along one side, a third treble staggered on the opposite flank. With modern lures deadbait spinning (as opposed to wobbling) is probably a method unlikely to be used much, if at all, although there is really no good reason why not, for it is very successful.

Fishing for fry-feeding pike is one of the most exciting and productive of pike-angling experiences. The pike themselves are not preoccupied with tiny roach fry, although as a rule they do prefer livebaits. The very best approach is to use a livebait larger than the fry, fished deep where the pike lie between striking. However, if a good livebait is not available, a bunch of small fish is a useful substitute. You cannot comfortably fish 2–4 livebaits on the same hook, because some will always be lost on the cast. The best hook rig is shown in Fig. 5 and consists of two or even three size 4 or 2 single hooks along the same trace, but at 180° to each other. All the hooks are firmly fixed in one plane, the trace wire simply being passed through the eye of the top hook, then wrapped 8–10 turns around the shank and on to the lower hook. One or two baits are put on each hook to create a constantly bustling mini-shoal.

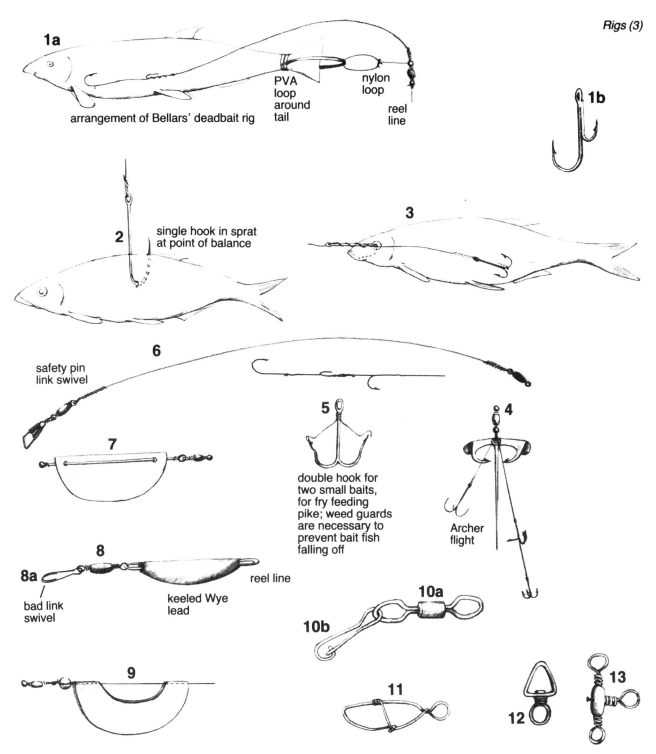

**1a**

arrangement of Bellars' deadbait rig

PVA loop around tail

nylon loop

reel line

**1b**

**2** single hook in sprat at point of balance

**3**

**6** safety pin link swivel

**5** double hook for two small baits, for fry feeding pike; weed guards are necessary to prevent bait fish falling off

**4** Archer flight

**7**

**8**

**8a** bad link swivel

keeled Wye lead

reel line

**10a**

**10b**

**9**

**11**

**12**

**13**

All pike fishing should be done with wire traces, and spinning is no exception. Spinning traces (see Fig. 6) need to be only 10 inches in length (long enough to wrap around the snout of a large pike, but not to bring the line in contact with the teeth), with a good swivel at one end and a link or snap swivel at the other end.

Fig. 7 shows the traditional anti-kink vane, consisting of a 1½-inch length of 20 s.w.g. wire, eyed at one end and with a swivel at the other. A crescent-shaped piece of clear perspex is mounted on the wire, which, by acting as a keel, enables the trace swivel to work correctly against a fixed point, thus preventing line kinks from travelling the length of the line. The reel line is tied to the eye of the vane, and the swivel is then attached to a 12-inch length of line which in turn is tied to the trace.

The anti-kink vane has no practical weight of its own. Fig. 8 shows what is known as a 'keeled Wye lead' which effectively incorporates an anti-kink vane plus some amount of lead to aid casting. In addition, we have shown what we consider to be a bad design of link swivel (Fig. 8a), from which lures/traces can easily detach. Preferred patterns of link swivel are shown in Figs 10 and 11.

The 'fold-over' lead (Fig. 9) is also a dated, though perfectly effective, method of adding weight quickly to a spinning tackle. It is simply a disc of sheet lead with a central hole cut away which is folded over the line up from the trace. The lead slides easily along the

25

line but can be locked in place with split shot. Adding lead to a spinning tackle aids distance casting, of course, but it also takes the lure rapidly to the bottom and, up to a point, keeps it deeper on the retrieve. However, this latter point depends very much on the depth of water and the length of the cast.

Swivels are especially important in piking for two reasons. Firstly, they are the only reliable method by which nylon line can be attached to the wire trace and, secondly, with particular techniques they can assist in keeping the line kink-free. Fig. 10a shows the design of (link) swivel we use in preference to any other. Marketed by Peter Drennan, it is called the 'diamond-eye' swivel. In sizes 8–12 we have found this pattern to be thoroughly reliable. Fig. 10b shows the pattern of link which we also like. It consists of a spring clip which retains the lure, or whatever, quite positively.

Fig. 12 illustrates a very simple, but reliable and strong, diamond eye link which is perfectly good enough when attaching reel line and trace wire, and can be used when swivels are simply not needed— such as on deadbait traces. We would suggest the wire is twisted to the circular eye, and the nylon to the diamond eye, which centralises the knot.

Many years ago three-way swivels (see Fig. 13) were used in paternoster tackles. We do not feel that they are essential, although we do not reject them out of hand. The paternoster link must be tied to the side eye, and the reel line and trace to the top and bottom eyes respectively. Sharpe's ball bearing swivels are the *crème de la crème* of swivels; they are expensive and hard to find but they will eliminate line kinking on spinning tackles, or deadbait wobbling rigs, without the need for anti-kink vanes.

# RIGS (4) DEADBAITS

There are as many rigs for deadbaiting as there are species of fish for the same use. All have their advocates despite the fact that some rigs are genuinely better pike-takers than others. With today's enlightened attitude to piking and the acceptance of quick striking, a number of modern hook rigs are geared towards fast strikes. The use of barbless hooks also offers the questionable advantage of easy unhooking.

Collectively, we have around 65 years of piking experience and most, if not all, of these deadbait rigs have been tried (and, indeed, one or two invented), tested and in the majority of cases rejected. What a good hook rig requires is efficient bait coverage to enable a reasonably quick strike, and not so many hooks as to increase the risk of bait rejection and to make unhooking perilous for the pike.

Figs 1a–g trace historically the developments and changes in several types of pike deadbait rigs. Figs 1a and 1b show early arrangements used by Barrie Rickards and Ray Webb. In both cases the trace is threaded through at least part of the bait (and therefore effectively rules out frozen baits), which takes all the force of the cast. Only one treble hook is used for hooking the pike—the single hook in Fig. 1a is an additional casting aid—but on whole baits, such as herrings and mackerel, there is insufficient bait coverage to enable a quick strike unless you know how the pike has taken the bait. Fig. 1c is the arrangement offered by Fred J. Taylor (one of the pioneers of deadbaiting in recent history), consisting of two fixed trebles set towards the head, and wrong, end of the bait. Again, the trace is threaded through the tail of the bait and, although bait coverage is important, the fact that both hooks are forward in the bait means that it is effectively a deep hooking rig.

Figs 1d and e show the Dave Steuart multi-hook 'instant strike' rig which had many advocates in the 1960s and, indeed, its popularity may well have continued had it, too, not shown some faults. The first problem is that very few people have the courage to strike immediately a run or pick-up is registered (assuming that the bite indicator is even capable of showing the moment a pike has picked up the bait!), and removing six trebles from the throat, or gut, of a pike is a task beyond even the best of us. The second problem to emerge is that the pike did not like them! Fishing in hotspots with multi-hook rigs, and with simple tackles such as Fig. 1f, has proved conclusively that more runs come to baits with the fewest hooks and that dropped runs are also less common.

Nevertheless, it should be noted that rather than thread the trace through the bait, a large single hook pushed through the tail root gives all the support necessary for casting. This latter is a much improved arrangement, for not only is it much easier to bait up it also encourages the use of frozen baits.

The rejection of the multi-hook rig and the inefficiency of rigs a–c led to a rethink. Fewer hooks equalled more runs and the increasing preference for 'half-baits' (since Martin Gay started the ball rolling in 1963) enabled the use of simple, but very efficient, hook tackles. Fig. 1f is just one of these and consists of one treble hook positioned 4–5 inches along the bait from the tail. In this particular case the trace is threaded through the bait, but if a single size 2 hook is fixed to the trace about 4 inches from the treble, the rig is transformed to one which is simple to bait up and is a very good hooker.

Today we rarely use whole herrings or similar sized deadbaits, so the general principle in Fig. 1f is redundant. However, Barrie Rickards, who is constantly experimenting, prefers the time-honoured snap tackle. It consists of a fixed bottom treble and a sliding Ryder treble up-trace. This flexibility will accommodate, in an instant, larger baits than Martin Gay's rig can, although the principle is exactly the same. The 'Ryder' hook is placed in the tail root; the bottom hook, usually 4–5 inches away, is hooked near the base of the dorsal or, in the case of head halfbaits, through the lips and in the shoulder.

In recent years pike anglers have been treated to sophisticated electronic bite alarms, such as the Dellareed 'Optonic' and Eddie Turner's 'Backbiter'. Sensitive indicators and the much more widely accepted use of floats for all bait-fishing methods of piking have largely eradicated the fear of deep hooking. Nevertheless, there are some waters where the pike gulp the bait down quickly on the spot. This may have nothing to do with fishing pressure, or pre-baiting, but it does call for careful and watchful fishing. Clearly, the fewer hooks used the better, and the further back on the bait they (or it) are positioned, the less likely is deep hooking. Fig. 1g illustrates the idea of having the hook in the tail root.

Having said this, there is no substitute for awareness and tackle watching. There is no excuse for wandering away from unattended rods. Fishing with the line reasonably tight to the bait and using reliable and sensitive bite indicators should become second nature.

In all static deadbaiting methods we recommend using small hooks. Treble sizes should be 8 or 10, but if you prefer single hooks then sizes 6 and 8 are called for.

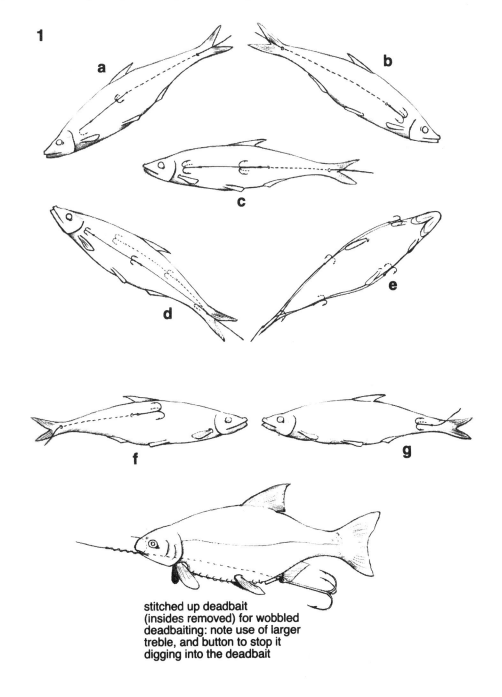

stitched up deadbait
(insides removed) for wobbled
deadbaiting: note use of larger
treble, and button to stop it
digging into the deadbait

# COVERING THE WATER

Effective coverage of the water is of paramount importance when it comes to catching pike consistently. Distance away from the bank, angle from the bank and depth within the chosen area: all must be tried. Today's pressure on fisheries has undoubtedly pushed a lot of fish to distant areas, although there is no question that a great many pike spend their lives in remote spots. This is especially relevant in shallow gravel pits and reservoirs where holding areas are just as likely to be found 200 yards out as close to the margins.

Using modern tackle and casting techniques baits can be cast to about 70–80 yards. In Fig. 1 we show what you might call a 'typical' gravel or clay pit with bankside points, and bars (submerged and islands) running the length of it. Swim X is clearly the best vantage point from which baits can be placed in several of the gulleys or adjacent to the bars. Almost irrespective of wind direction or strength, spots 1 and 2 are 'cast out' baits which take advantage of any pike patrolling the nearest bars and breaks along them. Assuming that the far bank is 'out of bounds', the top bay (3) cannot be fished, as a cast in excess of 130 yards is required to reach it. This particular bay is a pike-holding area where patrolling fish rest up during the late morning. Therefore, the only ways by which we can fish this area are either by boat (unlikely on most fisheries) or by making use of prevailing winds and drifting the bait by balloon or vaned float, or by using a combination of the two.

Area (4) is also a very long way from swim X and cannot be reached from the bank because of trees—some in the water—and islands which cut off access. Fortunately, a westerly wind blows directly into the hotspot and so it is very easy to drift a bait right under the fallen tree which hides most of the pike.

Locating 'text book' pike swims is achieved relatively easily by the above methods, although it can be time-consuming on a big water, and some trial-and-error approach is necessary. There is no easy alternative, any more than there is for the next problem, finding the correct depth. On shallow waters, even down to 10 feet, it is probably a good idea to fish the baits within the bottom 2–3 feet because any patrolling pike will still see them. In much deeper water of 20 to 40 feet the prey fish often 'hang' nearer the surface and sometimes within the top 4 feet, especially at dawn. Consequently, the pike are likely to be found beneath them, but in mid-water. Ledgered baits might, therefore, be a waste of time.

In Fig. 2 we show the standard paternoster on the marginal shelf (2a), with the bait close to the bottom in the deepest water (2b), and the standard ledgered bait at long range (2c). Although using a rather stereotyped approach, these techniques catch many pike on most shallow waters, still or flowing. We depict a boat for completeness and, of course, each of the methods can be used from it. Furthermore, where a boat channel is being fished it may be necessary to fish under the boats on ledger or sunken float rig.

Many fisheries have a shallow marginal shelf (or the margins of islands and bars) along which pike often patrol, or lay in wait, especially during quiet early mornings. In water of only 2 or 3 feet in depth a free lined or lightly ledgered livebait (see Fig. 3a) is as good a method (although a neglected one) as any. Later in the day when the pike move off-shore, but because of the roach shoals stay actively hunting near the surface, a paternostered livebait fished in the top half of the water and fixed in position amongst the pike will score heavily (see Fig. 3b). Paternostering a bait on a long lead link (upwards of 4 feet) presents problems, especially at long range when effective casting becomes impossible, or when the marginal shelf runs out a long way.

Accurate depth plumbing is less important when the precise feeding band is undetected, so a sunken float is used and a balloon employed to take the tackle to the required distance. At the specified range the balloon is struck off, after which the bait is fished in the usual fashion. To overcome the shallow margins and to prevent the paternoster link from fouling the weed, the link is loosely coiled and tied with PVA string. This material takes a short while to dissolve, by which time it is hoped that the balloon will be sufficiently far out for it not to matter!

Alternatively, a greased line float-fished livebait (see Fig. 3c), used without a vaned float, can be carried to distant areas with a balloon. After the balloon is released the bait will slowly cover the area rather than be carried away on the wind.

Deadbaits can, of course, be used with all the above methods. Fig. 4a shows the free-lined, close range deadbait on the shelf. We specify 'close range' because we suspect the bite detection efficiency of a long range free-lined deadbait. In Fig. 4b we illustrate our preferred approach either to a long range deadbait or when fishing a deadbait beyond a shallow and/or snaggy margin. The depth is plumbed accurately so that the float holds the line close to the surface, and on very shallow margins it is sometimes advantageous to grease the line to keep it on the surface.

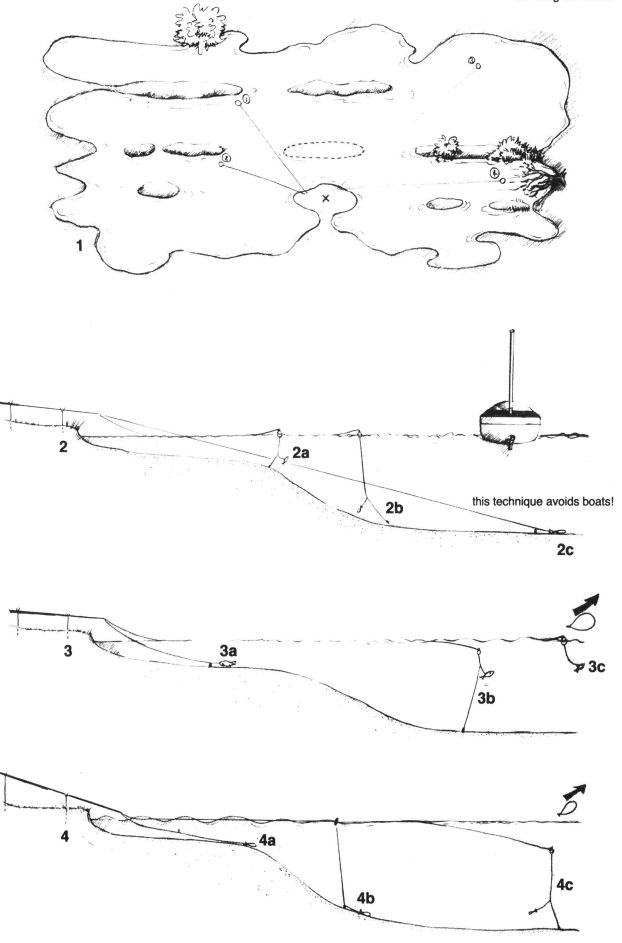

this technique avoids boats!

# BALLOONING

The problems associated with distance casting are well documented and present few real difficulties. Most anglers can cast a half-mackerel 50–60 yards, a few can reach 70 yards or so under good conditions, and with a strong back wind even greater ranges can occasionally be achieved. Beyond 100 yards it is virtually impossible to cast a pike bait without employing beach-casting tactics with 5–6 oz leads and shock-leaders, something many of us prefer not to do. So, we are left with how to get a good bait a long way—up to 200 yards—offshore. Fishing beyond casting range introduces a new set of problems for the pike angler, but the use of vaned float drifting techniques and ballooning overcome them all.

Several articles have appeared over the years outlining the ballooning technique, but so far each has failed to describe the inherent problems of terminal tackle/balloon tangling, and the balloon coming adrift on the 'cast' or, more correctly, the 'lob'. Fig. 1a illustrates the arrangement we have developed and currently settled upon. Starting above the trace we have the fixed lead, preferably $\frac{1}{4}$–$\frac{3}{4}$ oz in weight. Heavier weights than this impair the drift and often pull the tackle free of the balloon, although it is possible to go up to 2 oz. The lead must also be fixed to prevent it from sliding up to the balloon with the risk of tangling. To prevent the hooks from trailing back and bursting the balloon two adjacent split shots are fixed at a point rather more than the length of the trace up from the lead. A swivel is placed between them, the line running through one eye. To the opposite eye is attached the paper clip which holds the balloon. The paper clip should be at least 1 inch long. The reason we use the 'swivel-on-the-paper-clip' is to prevent, as far as possible, the line twist which results from the balloon spinning in the wind when the paper clip is fixed rigidly to the trace swivel (this is usually the method advocated). If a sliding float is used, it and the bead and stop knot are placed above the balloon.

In a strong wind, i.e. when there is no calm area close to the bank, the tackle is lowered into the water, the wind carrying the bait out to the chosen area. At the right point the line is checked, tightened up to the balloon, and a hefty strike pulls the balloon free. If the paper clip is attached to the trace swivel, the lead quite often tangles with it, which usually prevents the balloon from coming free on the strike (see Fig. 1b): there is nothing more frustrating than spending 30 minutes coaxing the bait out 180 yards only to find everything has to be retrieved because the balloon will not come free. And if this happens the reel line twists up badly.

Gentle winds produce calm areas along the bank, which may stretch out for 20 yards at times. Clearly the balloon cannot catch the wind, so the tackle must be lobbed out to the ripple line. If the balloon is just slipped into the paper clip, the weight of the bait usually pulls the balloon free before the tackle hits the water. This problem is simply overcome by tying the balloon quite firmly to the paper clip with PVA string. Thirty seconds after the drift has started the PVA dissolves.

We have described the vaned float drifting technique elsewhere. However, the tackle is cast directly from the rod, but if the float is set at, say, 15 feet and the margins at 3 feet run out for a greater distance than it is possible to cast, or if the margins are particularly snag-ridden which would prevent the drift, then you have problems. In Figs. 1d and 1e we show how easy it is to use a balloon in the aforementioned manner to tow the float out until the required point is reached, after which the balloon is again struck off. Fig. 1d shows the ET float, Fig. 1e the Colin Dyson pattern.

There are two final points to mention. After the balloon is inflated and knotted, the paper clip should be placed between the knot and the extreme end of the balloon but only if the latter portion has itself been twisted up to a string-like shape. Otherwise, the paper clip should go on the knot itself, which is the way we have illustrated it here. If the paper clip is simply attached between the knot and the aperture of the balloon, with neither of these precautions taken, the balloon comes off all too easily.

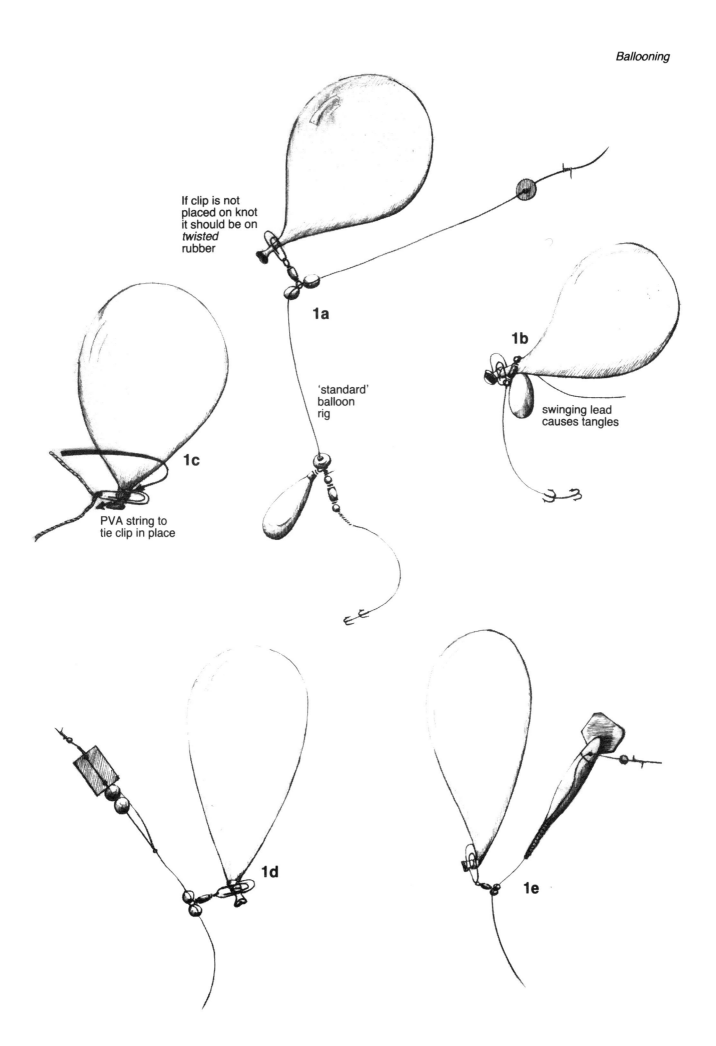

If clip is not placed on knot it should be on *twisted* rubber

**1a**

'standard' balloon rig

**1b**

swinging lead causes tangles

**1c**

PVA string to tie clip in place

**1d**

**1e**

# VANED FLOAT DRIFTING IN PRACTICE

With the wind blowing directly off the fishing bank and the pike holding area straight out in front, vaned float drifting is then in its simplest form. All that is needed is to cast into the ripple line and feed greased line to the float as required. However, the wind direction is rarely so amenable, or the pike sitting directly in front; more commonly the wind is at an angle to the fishing position, or the whereabouts of the pike unknown. It is in the latter situation when drifting really comes into its own and pike can be found with good water coverage.

In Fig. 1 we show the wind blowing directly from behind the angler, who is fishing from position 1. The cast is made slightly to the left of the fishing position, some loose line is paid out and the float is allowed to drift away for a distance of, say, 50 yards. If no take is forthcoming, the line is checked, thereby holding the bait in one fixed position for a short time. The second effect of checking the line is that it causes the float to move sideways. If no sideways drift comes 'naturally', the angler moves along the bank to position 2. He can now do one of two things: (1) by moving the rod, with the line paying out freely, he can keep the float approximately along the same line; and (2) by checking the line, the float will move to the right and inwards.

Once the new fishing position is reached, the drift is allowed to continue. In (1) this means that the float will drift away at an angle to the bank, whereas in (2) it will simply recommence a straight course. More line is given to the drift until, perhaps, 100 yards is paid out; then the procedure is repeated until the reel is almost empty. Sometimes, even when the wind appears to be blowing from directly behind, a different effect is noticed at range. Trees, buildings and natural bankside obstructions can all deflect the wind, as can bays and points on the water, and it may be that at long range the drift goes off to one side, thereby effectively improving water coverage in conjunction with the technique detailed above.

In Fig. 2 we show the wind blowing from the left and slightly off the bank. Once again fishing from position X, the cast is made upwind (that is, to the left) and some, though less, free line is offered to the drift. As soon as the wind has caught the vane, the float drifts to the right and away. At a point chosen by the angler the line is checked and, because the wind is at an angle to the bank, the tackle actually begins to drift inwards. Once more, when the angler chooses, free line is paid out and the drift away from the bank restarts. This can be repeated at regular intervals until the drift is complete, or preferably until a pike comes along!

Variations on both of these approaches can, of course, be employed, as can an unchecked drift to the horizon. The beauty of the method is that the angler's own intuition and inventiveness are the key to success.

One or two little gadgets make drifting more enjoyable, and the first of these is a reliable grease to keep the line on the surface. Apart from keeping the line above obstructions, a floating line helps the drift by reducing drag, and aids the 'mending' of line, which is often needed. For years we used 'Mucilin' brand line flotant, but recently 'ET Tackle' has introduced a superior grease under its own brand name.

'ET Tackle' also market a neat little 'auto-line greaser' (see Fig. 3a). It consists of a shaped duplon plug of 25 mm and 20 mm O.D. which fits into one of the butt rings. The central hole through which the line runs is packed with grease, thereby smearing the line on the way out and on the retrieve. Casting often dislodges the grease 'plug' so regular topping up is required.

When the float has drifted away upwards of 80 yards, and thereafter to perhaps 200 yards, the line has to climb over a deep lip of the fixed spool reel. Sometimes the towing effect of the float is insufficient to pull line from the spool, so the angler must keep an eye on things and pay out line by hand as required. Eddie Turner's piking colleague, Vic Gibson, has come up with the lazy man's alternative to this. It consists of a piece of wire about 4 inches long (see Fig. 3b) which is taped to the rear rod rest just below the reel and bent at right angles to the rod rest so that the pin faces upwards. Once the drift is underway the spool is removed from the reel, and is placed on the pin so that it can revolve easily, paying out line to the float. We do not use this gadget ourselves, preferring to pay out line by hand, but if you do adopt it remember to replace the spool before striking!

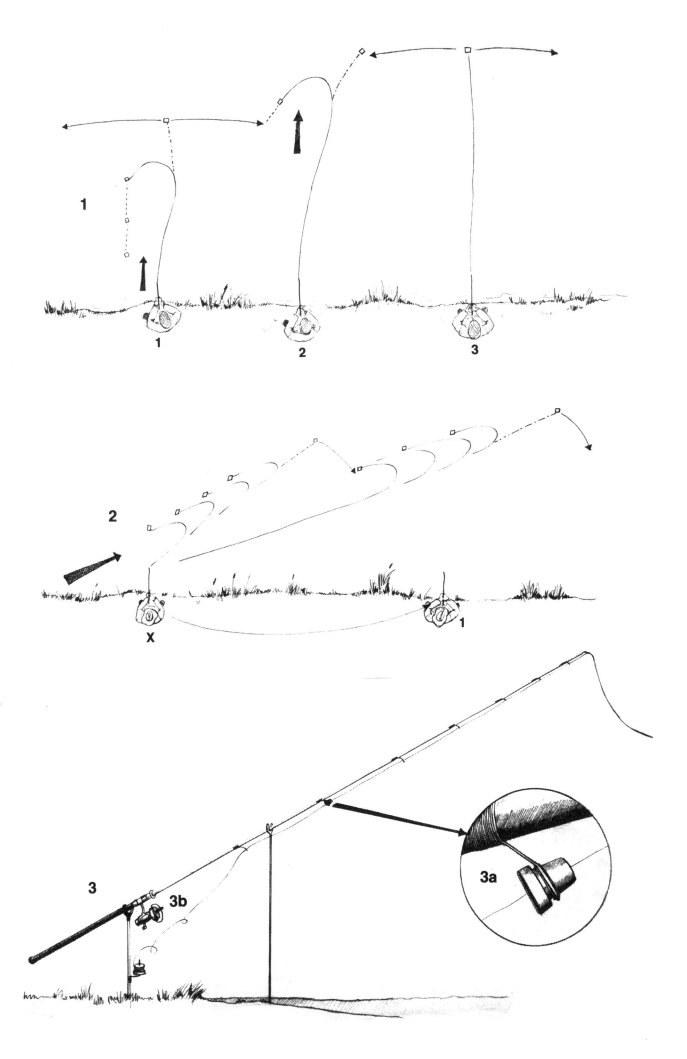

# TECHNIQUES (1)

In still waters the severest problem likely to be experienced is strong undertow, which on a big, deep and exposed water can reach such proportions as to drag a 1 oz lead and herring out of position. In some rivers the current will do this all the time; in others which are slower moving and deeper, and in drains, such conditions occur occasionally when the water is being pumped off or is in flood. Additionally, and particularly in drains (those which are normally still), pumping shifts a lot of rubbish, some of which is carried along the surface. In Fig. 1 we show the set-up which reduces the risk of surface flotsum catching the line, but at the same time keeps the bait clear of bottom snags and debris moving close to the bottom.

The rod tip is submerged by several inches to keep all of the line beneath the surface. The float, which is important in holding the bait up, is fished submerged so it, too, is clear of surface rubbish, whilst the paternoster link is long enough to keep the bait above the bottom rubbish. The paternoster lead needs to be sufficiently heavy to hold everything in place, but not so heavy as to hold position when, and if, rubbish does lodge on the line—you want to know this just as much as when a pike takes.

Holding position in a strong flow when the bait is being fished against the far bank is a problem solved in a quite different way. Fig. 2 shows the method, with the rod held as high as necessary to keep as much line as possible above the surface and, if you can, directly between the rod and the float—which this time is fished on the surface. Because the current dragging on the lead is so reduced, a surprisingly small amount of lead is often needed to hold position against the far bank, where the current can be slower.

Water resistance on the line is the biggest problem facing the river pike angler trying to hold position in the current. Reducing the resistance, therefore, is top priority in good fishing, and an effective way of doing this is to remove the float, reverting the tackle to the straightforward running, or fixed, ledger. Fig. 3, side elevation, details the standard arrangement for ledgered dead or livebaits. Fig. 3a shows the bow in the line which is the result of paying out a few feet of line, after the lead and bait have settled on the bottom, during across or normal downstream fishing. This line bow may reduce drag on the terminal tackle but it is still held under tension by the current. Fig. 3b shows how the rod tip is submerged for upstream casts which, coupled with the controlled amount of 'slack' line, is aimed at keeping the line as close to the bottom as possible to reduce line drag. The current tends to push the line to the bottom, rather than lift it as it does in downstream fishing.

It is a known fact that heavy undertow in still waters is caused during and for a while after a big wind, so if there are not enough problems keeping the tackle in place, the strong winds on rivers also frequently blow rods out of their rests. There are two very effective ways to combat this. The first, for gale force winds, is to angle the rod rests into the wind so that the wind effectively pushes the rod into the V-shape of the rod rest head, thereby keeping it in place. The second answer, for hurricanes, is shown in Fig. 4. The rod rest is kept in the usual upright position and a small elastic band is looped across its head over the rod, firmly holding the rod in place. It may be necessary to do this to both front and rear rests (if both are used!) Despite the claims by some anglers, there is *always* time to remove the bands before picking up the rod and striking; in fact, it is impossible to do otherwise!

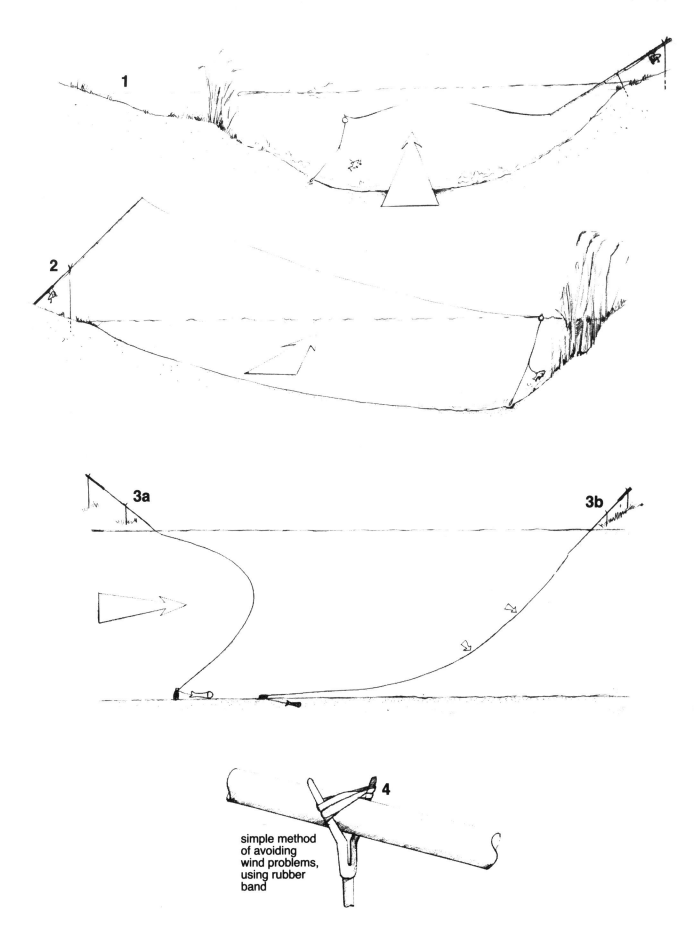

**1**

**2**

**3a**

**3b**

**4**

simple method
of avoiding
wind problems,
using rubber
band

# TECHNIQUES (2)

Fig. 1 depicts the standard float-ledgered deadbait, with the float-to-bait distance about 15 per cent greater than the depth of the water. The line between the float and the trace is inclined towards the surface, not overly tight, and because of the over-depth setting the float 'faces' the angler to show its colour to the best advantage. The line is tensioned between the float and the rod, this same tension supporting an indicator at the rod. The bait and trace lie flat on the bottom, tethered by a small amount to lead which further holds the line in tension. As the bait is picked up the tension is released, the float shifts position and, depending on whether the pike runs away from or towards the rod, the indicator at the rod either pulls free of the line clip or drops back as the line slackens.

The same technique, but used in a river, is shown in Fig. 2, although there are subtle differences. The 'trace' lead is necessarily heavier to hold in the current; the float-to-lead distance is greater, up to 50 per cent, to keep the float on the surface; and there has to be a bow in the line between the float and rod. As the bait is picked up, particularly if the lead is fixed, the float is likely to drop downstream a short distance before the pike moves off. Even if the pike swims towards the rod, slack line bites are not as common as in still water because the current takes up most of the slack, depending on the strength of the current and speed of the run.

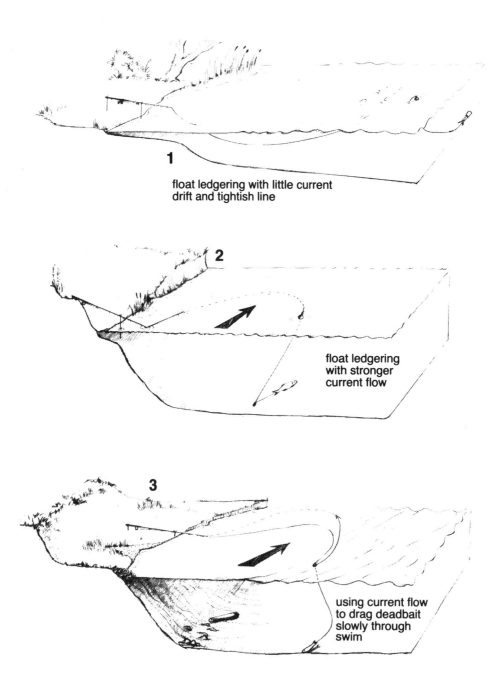

**1** float ledgering with little current drift and tightish line

**2** float ledgering with stronger current flow

**3** using current flow to drag deadbait slowly through swim

# TECHNIQUES (3)

For no apparent reason in some waters pike respond better to certain techniques than to others, and the *buoyant* ledgered deadbait is one such method. In Fig. 1 we show the technique in practice, with the addition of a float to keep the line clear of the slope and weedbeds. (*A word of warning*: be most careful not to inject, or indeed puncture, your own skin, as air in the blood supply can be deadly.) Just sufficient air (or buoyant material) is used to lift the bait lightly off the bottom. With a fixed lead the bait will rise only by the length of the trace, but with a sliding lead you can let out line to buoy the bait to any depth you require before clipping the line.

Buoyant baits can be used equally well over bottom weed or silt, but are just as effective—or useless— over a hard bed in still or moving water.

In Fig. 2 we show a ledgered (live) bait being held in position against a gentle flow, with the use of just sufficient lead to hold position comfortably. The bait is liphooked so that it rests head upstream, but because of the inevitable bow in the line caused by the current a reliable bite indicator system must be used since slack line bites may be the norm.

The free-lined livebait is a much neglected method today, probably because there is a widespread paranoia about fishing one's baits on the horizon. Similarly, it is distinctly unfashionable to use a shallow float-fished livebait. In Fig. 3 we show both methods used in a close range hotspot where the pike feed actively at all depths. With the free-lined bait the line should be kept under the slightest of tension after the cast is made and while the bait is swimming slowly to the bottom. Once the bait is resting on the bottom, tension the line only sufficiently to ensure good bite detection. Too much line resistance may induce the bait to swim towards the rod.

The shallow float-fished livebait is used under the smallest float capable of supporting the strongest efforts of the bait. The bait is likely to swim towards the surface so the line must be kept well greased and floating to prevent tangles and bite offs. Adding lead just above the trace will usually keep the bait within the depth band you have chosen but, if anything, may actually increase the risk of tangling if the line has sunk between the float and the rod, as the lead often causes the bait to swim eccentrically.

Tangling of the livebait with a sunken reel line is a common cause of bite offs and in Fig. 4 we show how easily it can occur. It is further compounded when using rudd livebaits because of their tendency to swim surfacewards. As they reach the uppermost limit of their travel (usually the length of the trace), the tether causes them to swim off-balance and as they sink back the hooks often foul the sunken line. This problem is especially relevant to dorsal hooked (about the point of balance) baits. However, a very easy and no less efficient way to hook any livebait, and rudd in particular, which almost totally prevents this, is to liphook it. If a second hook is used, such as with a snap tackle, then it is placed either in the dorsal region or preferably between the pelvic fins. A liphooked bait is not thrown off-balance, no matter in which direction it swims.

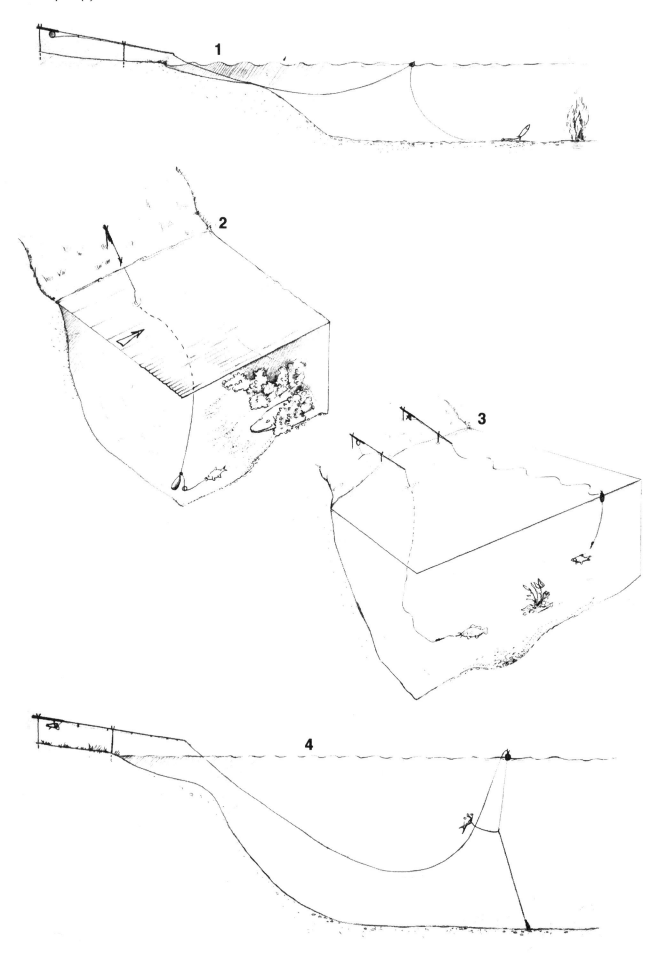

# FISHING SNAGGY SWIMS

We have covered some of the benefits of using a float for improved bite indication and as a means of presenting a bait in special circumstances. In addition to these benefits, the float is also used to keep line high in the water and clear of snags and weedbeds. In Fig. 1a we show the problem of ledgering, or free-lining, in the middle of rocks and sunken trees. Here, any slack line is carried by the current or drift among the snags, with the inevitable result. Fishing the bait on a tight line, either by keeping the line tensioned as the bait sinks or by tightening up after the bait has touched the bottom, offers no advantage as there can be no guarantee of keeping the line free of a snag at any stage in the proceedings.

The answer is to use a float set close to the actual depth of the water, with a sufficiently heavy lead to hold the bait in position against the current or drift. Fig. 1b shows this arrangement with a half mackerel.

When fishing in a moderate to fast flowing river or in a very heavy undertow, and only in these conditions, it may be necessary to increase the float depth setting to keep the float on the surface, and thereafter to use the current to keep the line under tension. Too little lead will enable the current to shift the bait out of position, and will continue to carry it until it finds a snag.

Fig. 1c outlines the general problem where too much line has been paid out to a float which is set over-depth. The slack line which results sinks, and there is a risk of it tangling with the snags. Where conditions permit, a further refinement is to grease the line to keep it right on the surface, but of course this may increase the risk of drag as the line is then right in the fastest water. A further problem depicted in Fig. 1c is that of using too long a trace: a short trace, as in Fig. 1b, is far less likely to find a snag than that shown in Fig. 1c.

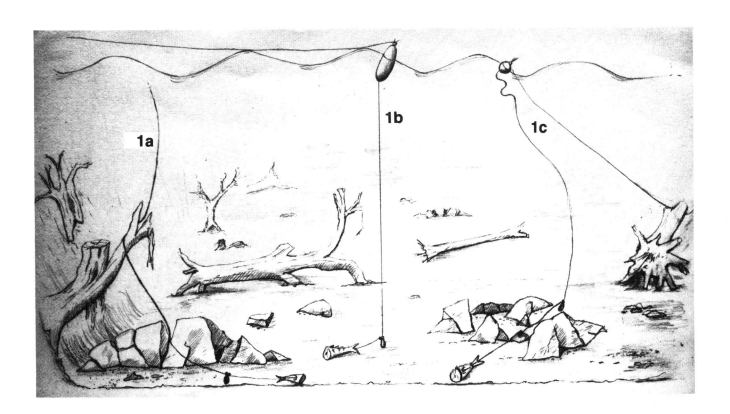

# WATER COVERAGE: RIVER AND DRAIN

Pike can be anywhere along a stretch of river, so it is important to cover completely all the points in a swim before moving along. In Fig. 1 we show the standard method of covering a river swim or drain. Bait position 1 is the closest to the angler, and is situated close to and just beyond the foot of the marginal slope, the bait being cast slightly upstream from the rod position. Position 2 covers the middle of the river (not always, but often the deepest part) where many pike are often found. This bait is cast straight out from the rod position, but should be moved about once per hour, moving in slightly closer each time until a new cast is needed.

On some rivers and, in particular, some drains the far bank (often the one not fished) has a steeper slope, which often means the pike are much closer to that bank. Subject obviously to the width of the river, it makes a lot of sense to place a bait along this far bank, and in bait position 3 we show the systematic way of fishing the area. It is especially useful if there is an inlet stream, culvert or eddy which may attract fry and pike.

If a third rod is used to fish the far bank, the bait should be angled downstream of the rod position so that any effect the current may have will be to take slack line downstream and away from the other rods. Rods 1 and 2 are fished on a shorter line and therefore are less troublesome if slack line is suddenly created.

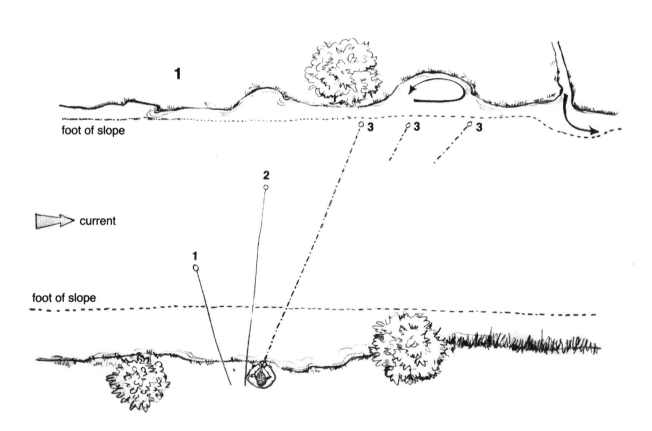

# SHALLOW-FISHED PATERNOSTER OVER DEEP WATER

In recent years we have become increasingly aware that pike at rest may actually spend much of their time in 'mid' water. On the other hand, hunting pike spend time looking for food quite near the surface, especially in the early morning when the prey fish shoals are high in the water. Float fishing a livebait in the suspected feeding zone is one way of catching these pike but drift or current may push the tackle into the margins and away from them. Clearly, this situation is one for the paternostered bait, a method which will hold the bait in a fixed position and, subject only to the length of the trace, within the suspected feeding zone. However, the bait can be fished no more than 4 feet or so off the bottom because

of the problems of casting a long paternoster link. Fig. 1a shows the simplest way to paternoster a bait up to 15 feet off the bottom, and involves coiling the paternoster link and tying the coils with PVA string or tape.

After the cast the PVA dissolves and the coils straighten out as the lead sinks in the usual fashion. It should be noted that whenever a livebait is fished close to the float (and in the case of this paternoster rig it is likely to be within 2 or 3 feet), the line between the rod and the float must be kept well away from the bait to prevent it from swimming up and over the line. The resulting tangle almost always results in a 'bite off' in the event of a take.

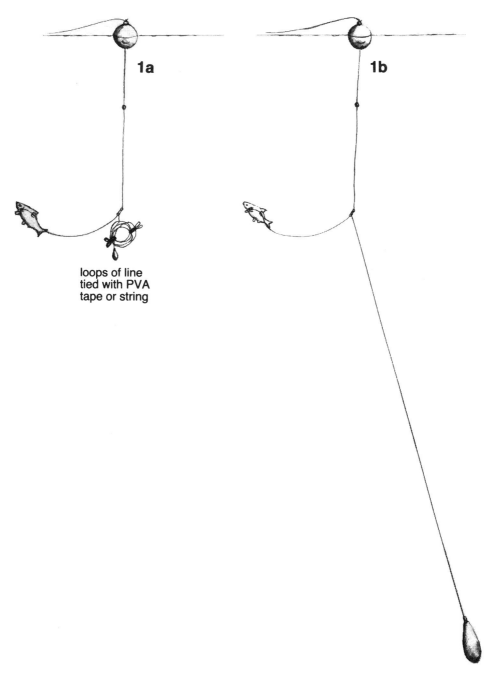

**1a**

**1b**

loops of line
tied with PVA
tape or string

# BAIT TROLLING

Some of the most enjoyable, and at the same time, productive pike fishing we have experienced has been trolling float-fished livebaits and deadbaits along the Wroxham to Horning stretch of Norfolk's river Bure. Of course this is not a method for rivers only. Indeed, boats permitting, livebait trolling is a highly efficient pike-taking method on any appropriate water, and there are few which are not suitable.

The technique is as follows. The area, or stretch of water to be fished, is plumbed reasonably accurately and the float-to-trace swivel distance is set to the correct depth. Depending on the size of bait and the speed of the current (if any), a suitable weight of fixed lead is placed directly above the trace. We would suggest that initially, with baits of about 4 oz, a half-ounce drilled bullet should be used. The line is greased, partly to keep the line on the surface but mostly because a floating line will more efficiently follow the path of the boat and will be easier to control if the end tackle needs to be moved quickly.

Once over the fishing area the baited tackle is lowered from each side of the boat (if two rods are to be used) or stern (for one rod). While paying out line the boat is rowed 15 to 30 yards, or more if wished, away from the float. At this point the reel is engaged, so trapping the line, and the boat is rowed at slow walking pace along the 'swim'. With the float behind the boat and the rowing angler facing backwards, 'takes' are seen quickly, the float almost always sinking from sight or travelling quickly sideways. There is rarely any doubt, but when the take does come stop rowing, lower the anchor quietly and quickly, pick up the rod and treat the 'run' in the usual manner. Some anglers, when using a fixed spool reel, prefer to leave the pick-up open and to hold the line in a clip. Although there is absolutely nothing incorrect in this, we have not found it necessary. We either use a multiplier or, with a fixed spool reel, engage the anti-reverse.

Fig. 1a shows the simple tackle arrangement and Fig. 1b the rod in the outrigger, with the bait trolled a few yards behind the boat. A rod placed in an 'outrigger' rod rest enables the bait to be fished much closer to the bank, but if you are fishing along the fringes of trailing tree branches it is often a good idea to have two anglers in the boat, one seated in the stern facing forwards as a guide, and the rower watching the floats. Two rods can be fished very effectively on outriggers, even with two anglers aboard: one rod fishing the margins, the other in open water. When the chosen stretch of water has been covered the boat should be turned around and a repeat run made so that both anglers fish the area equally but also because pike will often take on the second run.

We suggest rowing at a slow 'walking' pace and setting the float to the depth of the water because it has worked well for us, but obviously conditions on the day may suggest changing one or both. A quicker rowing speed will lift the bait higher in the water, as will less lead; too deep a float setting will cause the bait to snag the bottom more frequently.

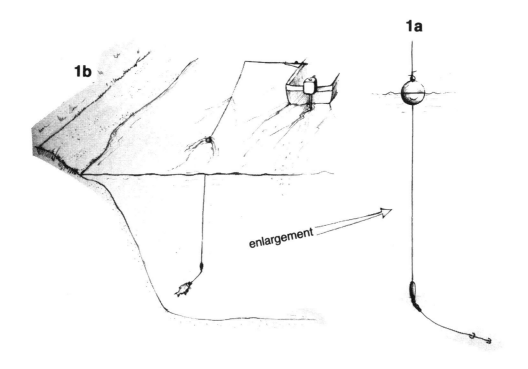

enlargement

# RISING FLOAT
# SUB-SURFACE PATERNOSTER

See Figs 1a–c. We have Vic Bellars to thank for this rig, which was devised to fish a bait on paternoster tackle (and therefore is fixed in one position and at one depth) well off the bottom over deep water. In practice there is no limit to the depth of water in which the bait can be fished; the only real limitation is the size, and strength, of the bait which can be lifted up by the sliding float as it rises to the surface.

Since the bait, float and lead are concentrated at the terminal end of the line, casting is reasonable, although a fairly heavy lead is best used to give the cast some direction (in flight both the float and bait slide up the line, thereby increasing wind resistance, so

long casts are not really possible). The tackle is fished under some tension, which means that even when the float is deliberately fished on the surface (and, of course, it does not need to be) an indicator at the rod is required because the drag will often just submerge the float.

As with the sunken float paternoster, of which this is but a variation, there is an ever present risk of a livebait tangling with the reel line, but there is nothing that can be done about it. With the trace running freely on the line, at least up to the stop knot, this is likely to happen less frequently than when it is fixed.

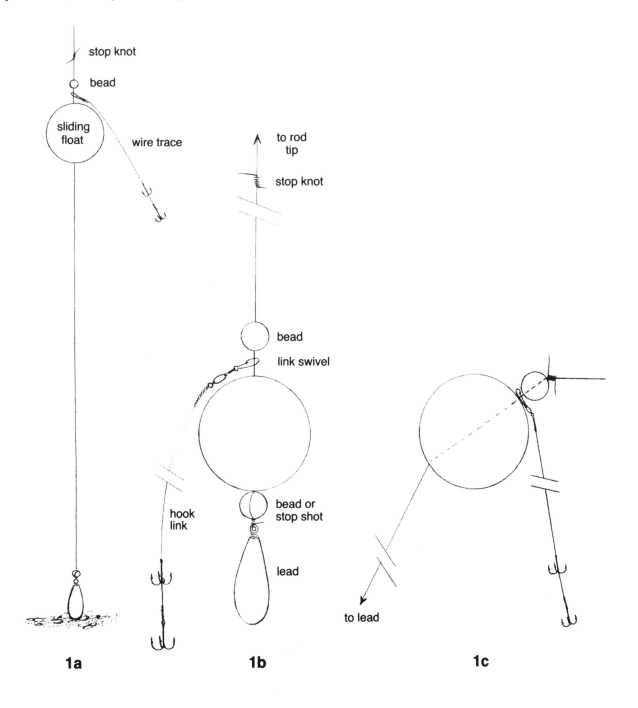

1a     1b     1c

# SUNKEN FLOAT PATERNOSTER

In recent years this method has become increasingly popular, though the reasons for it are obscure. The sunken float is in practice a sunken 'buoy' used to keep the bait clear of the bottom at a chosen depth. The float is therefore not used as a bite indicator; that has to be taken care of by indicators at the rod. As can be seen from the diagram the float is fixed close to the bait, and rather unlike the standard float paternoster rig (when the float is on the surface) the whole system is fished on a tight line. Beyond that the method has little to benefit it over the previously mentioned standard float paternoster.

The tight line increases the risk of a livebait swimming over the reel line, with the inevitable consequences when a pike strikes. This problem, and

a wish to separate further the bait from the terminal tackle, is why Colin Dyson devised the rig seen in Fig. 1. The diagram is self-explanatory, but it is worth mentioning that the distance between the 'float' and the trace swivel must be greater than the length of the trace so that the bait cannot hook up the float—which is a common cause of tangles in paternoster rigs. The tackle is fished under less tension than usual, which is better sense. However, an indicator at the rod is still required, and one that must detect slack line takes.

For reasons that are unclear, baits fished on this rig rarely tangle, which is a major step forward. The rig can be used to fish baits up to 6 or 7 feet off the bottom —as much as can comfortably cast with 11-ft rods while the paternoster link remains at a fixed length.

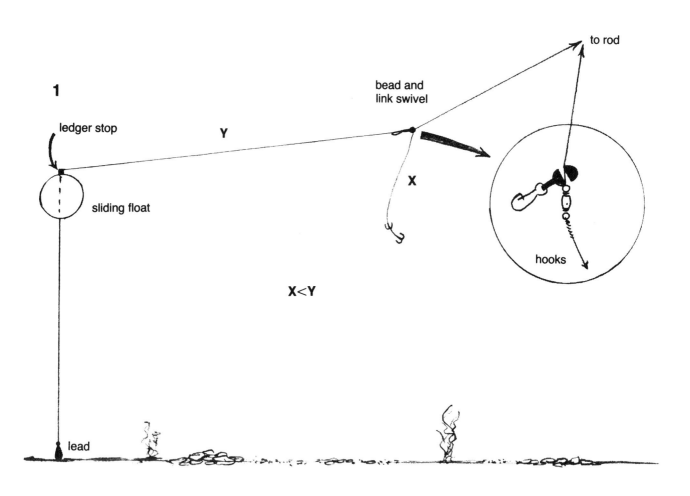

# STORING LIVEBAITS

Owing to unfounded concern about the spread of fish disease, the majority of water authorities, and an increasing number of angling clubs and associations, now prohibit the movement of livebaits between waters. In other words, livebaits may be used only on the waters from which they were caught. Needless to say, this may severely restrict pike angling activities, especially when baits have to be caught prior to pike fishing. In the autumn when pike usually feed most readily during the first few hours of light, any success with bait catching is rather limited by the fact that the pike have gone off the feed before they can be used. Clearly, some method of retaining livebaits over several days is called for so that, for example, an afternoon can be spent catching a few dozen baits which can then be stored at the fishery for later use.

The methods we discuss can be used with equal effect in the garden pond, and as a back-up in tubs and troughs behind the garage!

Fig. 1 shows a 5-gallon polythene tub, closed at either end and with numerous holes drilled in it to allow free passage of water through the tub. A three-sided flap is cut in one end to permit access to the baits. In cold water twenty 3 oz baits can be safely stored almost indefinitely.

Improved water flow, which in turn increases the number of baits that can be stored safely, is achieved with a cylindrical wire cage, 3 feet long, as shown in Fig. 2. A securely fastened door is needed for bait access and the entire cage is lowered on a rope into the water. Unlike the polythene drum in Fig. 1, this form of cage is prone to eel attention.

Fig. 3 illustrates perhaps the best of all livebait keeps, and consists of a wooden box 3 ft × 18 in × 18 in and a well-fitting padlocked lid. Holes drilled in all four sides ensure free passage of water. Polystyrene fixed to the lid provides insulation against sudden air temperature fluctuations. This is important because the box floats in the water, tethered to a firmly fixed stake. To improve the temperature stability further of the water around the box, and to protect it from frost and strong sunlight, the very best location is under an overhanging tree (see Fig. 4). Even beneath a bare tree in winter the water is somewhat protected.

Stored baits can be fed with trout pellets if kept for any appreciable length of time, but food demands and general activity are subdued by keeping the baits in a darkened environment, such as in the box described. Staked out keepnets offer none of the advantages of the box or the polythene tub and invariably result in frayed fins and worn snouts as the fish try to escape. Keepnets are best avoided in all bait-snatching activities: the baits are far healthier if on catching they are placed directly into a bucket.

If you do keep livebaits away from the fishery you will need something in which to carry them on the day. In Fig. 5 we show the readily available polythene bucket which is fine on the bank but needs a closely fitting lid for transportation in a car. In the same diagram you can see the excellent Shakespeare battery powered oxygen pump which can comfortably maintain up to twenty 4 oz fish in 3–4 gallons of water for a few hours. A second model of pump is now available which runs directly from the car cigar lighter via an adapter.

E.T. tackle sell a cylindrical metal cage which fits inside a standard 5-gallon bucket. All you do when arriving at the swim is lift out the cage containing the baits and place it in the water, tying it to a suitable stake. If the cost is too much, the same result is achieved by stretching a knotless mesh across the mouth of the bucket and securing it with an elastic retaining strap.

The good exchange of water keeps the baits fresh, but maintain a watchful eye on the bucket if a strong wind is blowing into your bank because a heavy surge can push it into very shallow water.

Transporting the baits in the car is best done in a 5-gallon bucket, half-filled with water, with tightly fitting, snap-on lid. Stand it in a large bowl to catch any spills.

1

**2**

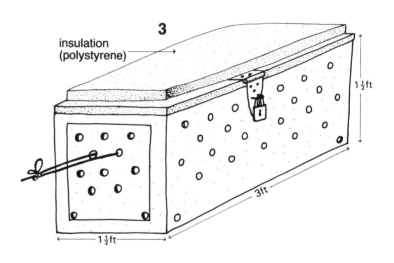

**3**

insulation
(polystyrene)

1½ ft

3ft

1½ ft

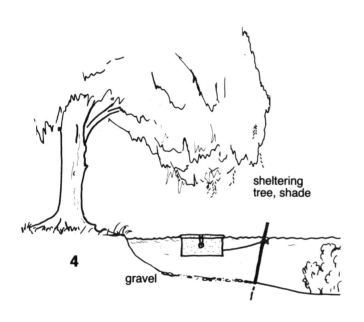

**4**

sheltering
tree, shade

gravel

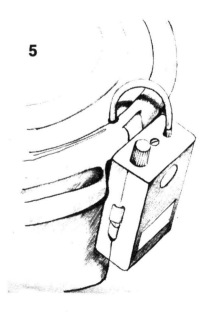

**5**

# PRE-BAITING AND GROUND-BAITING

If you trace pike angling history to the 1960s, you will detect a general concern among anglers that throwing in left-over deadbaits induces the pike to swallow baits on the spot, thereby leading to deep hooking problems. This concern still exists today.

Some pike do, indeed, swallow baits quickly, many of them on waters 'new' to deadbaiting, so clearly the problem is not one of inducing over-confidence but of not using a sensitive bite indication system. Neville Fickling, the authors and others have been experimenting over a number of years with pre-baiting for pike. Neville, on the one hand, pre-baits chosen swims with sometimes large quantities of dead fish; on the other, the authors regularly introduce fish sections and rubby dubby on the day of fishing.

The conclusions reached from both approaches are almost identical: that pike can be attracted to suitable areas, or at least held for longer periods, and at times they can be brought back on feed when there may

otherwise have been a lull. We often slice up frozen mackerel, sardines, herrings and sprats, allow them to thaw slightly, and hurl them out as soon as they will sink—frozen deadbait discs float, and will be carried away on the wind or by the current.

As well as attracting pike by the scent in the oils given off, introducing fish whole, or in sections, also feeds the pike and, if enough is put in, a noticeable increase in weight is recorded. In the figure we show an alternative way of introducing scent but less food. Quite simply, any surplus frozen deadbaits are thawed until they are 'crispy', at which point they are minced up and mixed with a proprietary groundbait. The mix is then rolled into hand-size balls, weighted with a stone, and these can be frozen for the future or taken to the swim and used immediately. A beautiful oil slick results as soon as the ball hits the water, the particles sinking, slowly dispersing and hopefully attracting pike to your whole or half deadbait.

# LURE FUNCTION CHART

Complicated as it may look, our flow diagram (opposite), or more correctly lure function chart, is self-explanatory. We show the section of water covered by specific designs of lure (spinners, spoons and plugs), and detail the diversity of patterns and highlight how almost any depth of water which can be fished can be effectively covered—even if that means using a perk or jig!

We mention specific patterns and marketing names as a guide to the range, but we should state that there are many other differently named models which duplicate those we highlight. Even so, it would be correct to say that some of the most successful lures are included in our list.

Floating plugs which dive to 3 or 4 feet (such as Rappalas) cannot effectively, or ideally should not, be used in greater depths by weighting the line. It is far better to select either a deep diving plug (e.g. deep diving River Runt) in moderate depth water of 8 to 12 feet, or a fast sinker (e.g. Rappala Deep Diver) in greater depths, bearing in mind that the retrieve will bring the plug towards the surface throughout the retrieve. Alternatively, a spoon (e.g. Toby) can be selected and it can be retrieved at most chosen depths. Delay the retrieve until the spoon has sunk to a predetermined level: cast out and count the seconds until the spoon hits the bottom, say 25 seconds. Counting 12 seconds on the next cast means the spoon is in mid-water, and so on.

To a certain extent the depth at which a spoon has to be retrieved depends on its weight. For example, a heavy spoon can only be retrieved at a shallow depth if done quickly. Therefore, it is sensible to carry the same pattern of spoon at different weights: lightweight for shallow retrieves, heavyweight for slow, deep retrieves, etc.

'Fly spoons' and 'bar spoons' (Mepps, Ondex, etc.) are generally shallow-water spinners, but Devon Minnows, because of their centrifugal effect, will hold a chosen depth a little better.

The illustration details basic types of spinner and spoon and, as with the previous comments, should be taken only as general guide lines. As the flow chart shows, the lure angler wishing to cover all eventualities should carry a representative selection of plugs and spoons, not only in various weights and sizes, but colours also. It is impossible to give all-embracing colour guides because there are so many variables: water clarity, light intensity, light penetration, depth of water and the pike themselves. However, we can give some guidelines.

Spinners—blade colour, silver/red, black/gold; minnows: green/gold, red/gold.

Spoons—silver, copper, copper/silver, silver/blue.

Plugs—white/red head, black, yellow, perch scale.

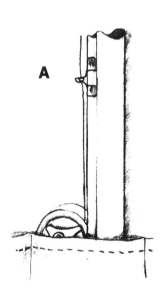

**A**

Holdall arrangement (A and B) for made-up rods, reel spools and lines.

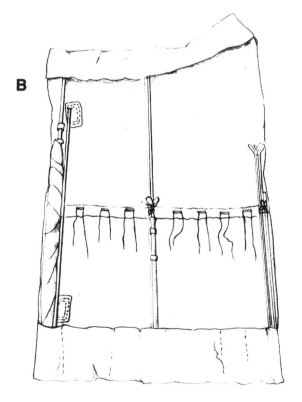

**B**

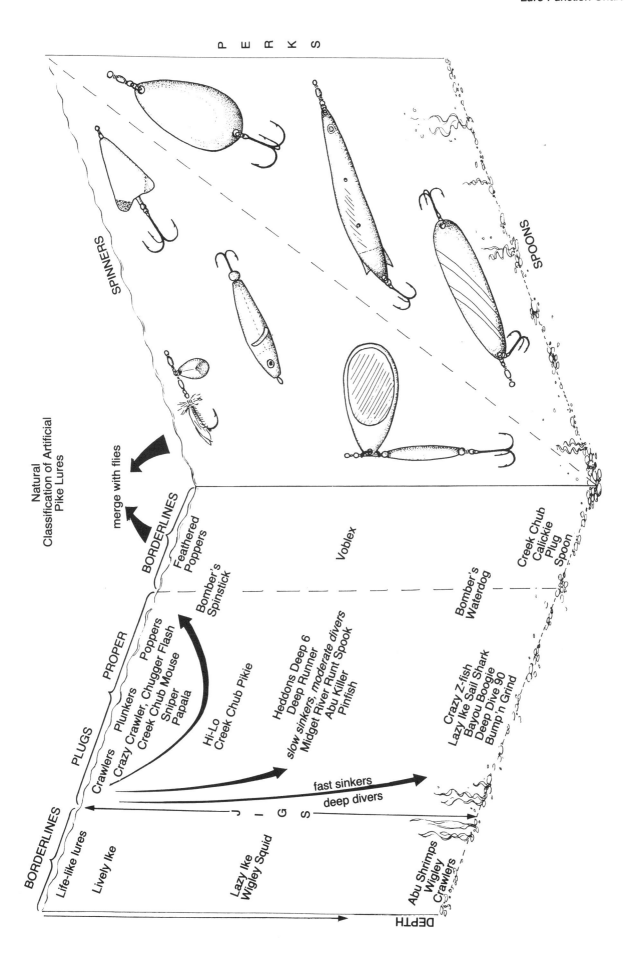

Natural
Classification of Artificial
Pike Lures

# SPINNERS AND SPOONS: BASIC PATTERNS

Jim Vincent, a successful Norfolk pike angler, gave his name to a large, lightweight spoon after having had considerable success with the pattern on the shallow Broads of his native county. Fig. 1a depicts the outline: a swivel at the narrower (front) end and a large (size 2) treble at the other. The lure can be fished easily in shallow water, with either a continuous or erratic retrieve.

George Higgins and his friends in Northern Ireland have certainly equalled Vincent's success on trolled spoons of the pattern shown in Fig. 1b. It is rather more squat, and gives a slightly 'sharper' action, the heavier gauge sheet metal taking the spoon to greater depths more easily than the Norfolk pattern. Going one stage further, Gordon Burton from Southport, among other successful lure anglers, has simply adapted the ordinary tablespoon. He has cut similar shapes and sizes (see Fig. 1c) from sheet alloy, and beaten them with a metal-working hammer to give the concave cross-section as shown in Fig. 2. Each of the three patterns, by using modern alloys or metals, can be constructed in various weights and colours. Brass, copper and 'silver' are the commonest colours, though the spoons can be painted; tassles can also be added to the hooks.

Fred Wagstaffe and Bob Reynolds, fishing Broadland in the late 1960s using spoons similar to the one in Fig. 1a, discovered that quite a number of pike actually struck at and missed the spoon when armed with just one rear treble. They improved the hooking success by attaching a treble to the front end and a second rear trailing hook on a short wire trace of about 1–2 inches. The spoon was named the 'Commando'. Figs 3a and 3b show the Abu 'Toby' spoon, a pattern which has actually been copied by several manufacturers. It is available in several weights, finishes and colours, and although not an especially good fish catcher it is certainly worth keeping a small stock. The eccentric design gives a good, erratic dance on retrieve. Its biggest problem is that even in small sizes it is quite heavy and demands a fairly rapid retrieve—something not always required, particularly in shallow water.

As takers of large pike, spoons are probably better than spinners, especially the patterns in Figs 1a–1c. However, there are notable exceptions to this and it must be said that spinners in all their patterns are excellent pike lures when sport, and not size, is what matters. Martin Gay has had considerable success on small Mepps red/silver 'spinners'; Barrie Rickards took lots of pike in his early years using the humble mackerel spinner (see Fig. 7). Fig. 4 shows the standard Mepps type ('Ondex' is another) bar spoon. It is available in several sizes and colours, casts well and can be fished at a variety of depths and speeds. A steady retrieve is best, and an anti-kink vane must be used.

Pike historians will remember the kidney spoon in Fig. 5. The name comes from the shape of the revolving blade, and although it is only a variation on the Mepps-type lure it was generally available in quite large (2″ blade) sizes. The outside surface of the blade was highly polished silver, the concave surface being painted red. Often the hooks would carry a red wool tag.

Of similar vintage, though different design, is the 'Colorado' spoon detailed in Fig. 6. The revolving body consisted of a spoon-shaped blade, with the addition of two eccentric blades which caused the blade to revolve around a central shaft. Colours were the same as the kidney spoon and it kinked line beautifully! It was a large and heavy lure and, in our experience, was not a good pike taker, and it certainly was not as productive as the mackerel spinner.

Mackerel spinners themselves were dull silver in colour and were featherweight. Here, of course, may be the answer to explain their greater success. About 1¼ inches long, the blade again revolved around a central shaft, and although it revolved rapidly on a steady retrieve its lightness allowed easier fishing over weed beds and just under the water surface.

The celebrated 'Devon Minnow' (Fig. 8) completes this introduction to basic lure types, and is perhaps best known as a salmon and trout lure. The body, available in several sizes up to 4 inches, is hollow and carries two offset vanes which cause the body to revolve about a central trace. This spinner—which also kinks the line badly without an anti-kink vane or reversible fins—is available in several 'two-tone' colours, such as red fading into gold, black/gold, etc. and in modern plastics makes a reasonable shallow water lure which casts very well indeed.

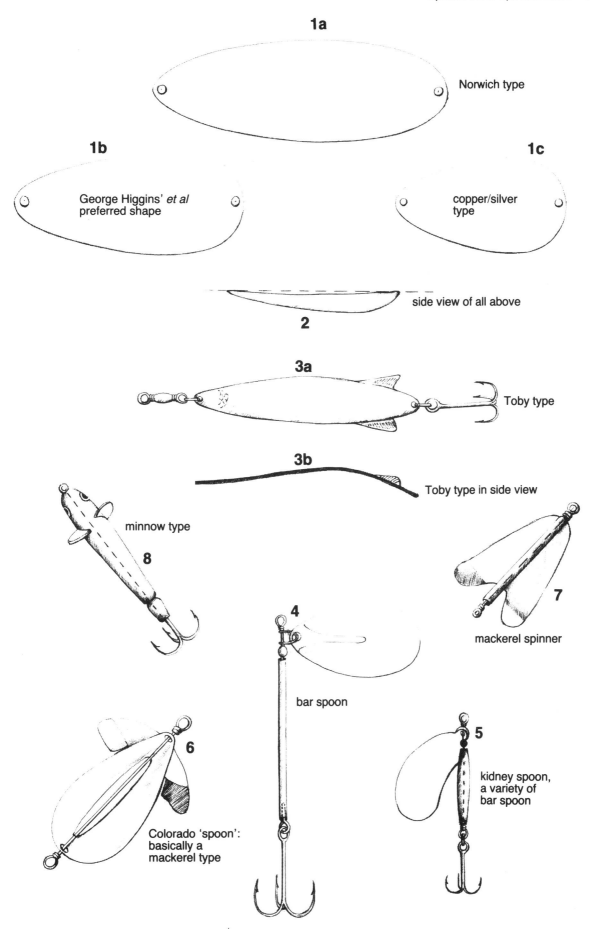

**1a**

Norwich type

**1b**

George Higgins' *et al* preferred shape

**1c**

copper/silver type

side view of all above

**2**

**3a**

Toby type

**3b**

Toby type in side view

minnow type

**8**

**7**

mackerel spinner

**4**

bar spoon

**6**

Colorado 'spoon': basically a mackerel type

**5**

kidney spoon, a variety of bar spoon

# CARRYING LURES

Most lures carry one treble hook, many carry two and some three, and it is these hooks and the need for lures to be readily to hand that gives the spinning enthusiast the headache of how and in what to carry them.

Treble hook guards are now available which satisfactorily prevent lures from tangling together, and as a result several lures can be carried safely in a jacket pocket, but clearly these numbers are limited. A few more, suitably hook guarded, can be carried en masse in a Tuppaware box, but there is a risk of damage to individual lures. Compartmental plastic boxes are better and are a good way for the bait fisherman to carry a few plugs, etc. in his rucksack; they are not satisfactory for the lure enthusiast.

Cantilevered 2 and 3 tray 'lure' boxes, as popularised in the United States, are common, and are actually quite useful in a boat, being waterproof, strong and offering easy access to the lures. On the bank they are a confounded nuisance, easily left in the last swim, and usually too small to carry a flask, camera, and so on. Those that will contain everything are too big!

Because of these general inadequacies Barrie has designed a lure roll which is incorporated into a useful haversack. It is large enough to carry some personal effects as well as a balance, camera, etc. Figs 1a and 1b show the bag closed, and the lure roll rolled out. The hooks are left attached to the lures which are 'hooked' between a wire spring on each side of the roll. As the roll is rolled up each turn of the canvas protects one lure from the next. No tangling, ready access to the lures, a useful haversack and a comfortable shoulder strap make this item the ideal lure angler's bag.

### Making Spoons and Spinners at Home

See Fig. 2. Very simple, though thoroughly effective spoons can be made easily from household tablespoons and teaspoons. The handle is cut off and the spoon smoothed of any jagged edges. A small hole is then drilled at both ends, each to take a small, strong, stainless steel split ring, one for the treble hook, the other for the trace connecting swivel. It is essential that these two holes are drilled along the axial line. If one is off-centre the spoon may spin, instead of wobbling.

'Jim Vincent' spoons (see Fig. 3), which are more elongated than the tablespoon lure, can be made with a little more work from sheet copper, brass or alloy. A master template is used to mark out the shape of the spoon on the sheet, which is then cut out with a hacksaw or tin snips (depending on the gauge of the metal) and filed smooth. Any concave/convex shape is achieved with a ball-hammer, which also adds a scale pattern to the surface. Once the desired shape is achieved the two holes are drilled, as in Fig. 2.

Fig. 5 shows a mackerel spinner and bar spoon respectively in exploded view. Parts for these basic styles of spinner can be purchased from Tom C. Saville of Nottingham, and are particularly easy and cheap to make.

Fig. 6 illustrates what the Americans call the 'Buzzin Bug'. In Britain its name is the 'Buzzer', and it is imported by Ryobi Masterline of Tewkesbury. As peculiar as it may look, it has proved a deadly pike lure for Barrie and is easily made at home. The V-shaped wire, looped at the apex of the 'V', is 24 gauge stainless wire. The hook is a large single (but can just as easily be a treble) and is concealed inside the 'streamer', which also hides a ¾ inch barrel lead. To the opposite arm of the 'V' is attached a swivel and one-inch spoon blade. The angle of the 'V' can be changed to suit fishing depth and, as an additional bonus, because the lure does not actually spin, there are no line kinking problems. It casts extremely well.

Commercially manufactured plugs (see Fig. 4), of hollow plastic or wood, have one inherent problem: that of insecure treble attachment. The tiny screw eyes, or screws, used can easily strip from the plug body, resulting in the loss of a pike. In this figure we show, without the need for much explanation, a home-produced means of very secure treble attachment. The central, axial hole must pass through the exact centre of the plug body otherwise the action will be lost, but once achieved the trebles cannot come adrift.

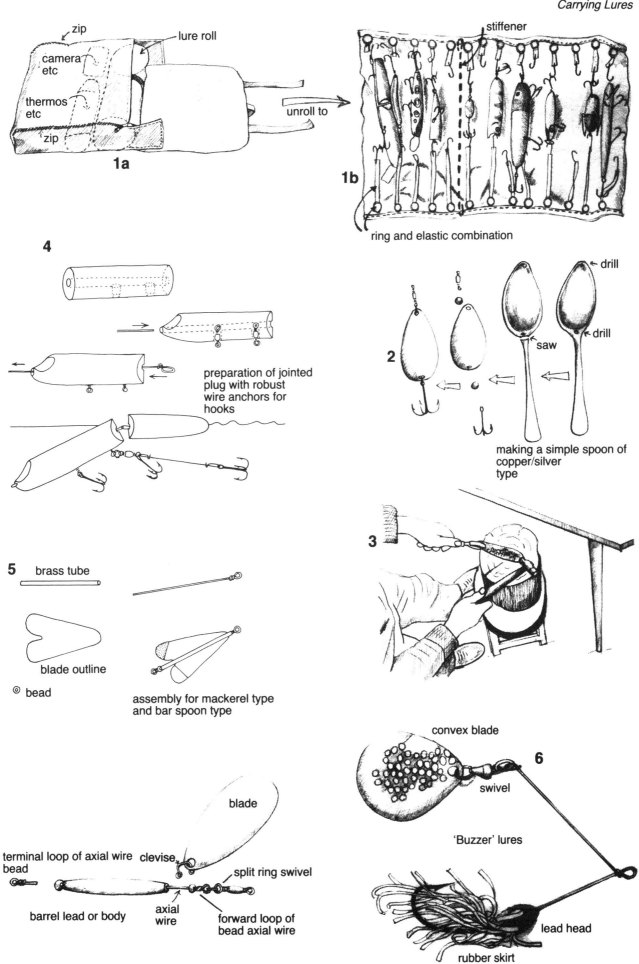

**1a**

zip

lure roll

camera etc

thermos etc

zip

unroll to

**1b**

stiffener

ring and elastic combination

**4**

preparation of jointed plug with robust wire anchors for hooks

**2**

drill

drill

saw

making a simple spoon of copper/silver type

**3**

**5**

brass tube

blade outline

© bead

assembly for mackerel type and bar spoon type

blade

terminal loop of axial wire

bead

clevise

split ring swivel

barrel lead or body

axial wire

forward loop of bead axial wire

convex blade

**6**

swivel

'Buzzer' lures

lead head

rubber skirt

# BOAT FISHING

Many pike anglers shun boat fishing and in so doing miss out not only on a very pleasant way of fishing but also on an entirely new approach to a water. There is no doubt that one's attitude changes dramatically as soon as casting limitations cease to matter and access becomes available to all parts of the fishery. Indeed, there are few more enjoyable ways of spending a pleasant autumn day than afloat, perhaps trolling a livebait along the margins of an island or watching a deadbait float bobbing in the waves on some distant shelf.

But all is not bliss. In heavy rain you and your tackle get wet, so proper waterproof clothing is essential. In a biting easterly wind you grow cold and even the best thermal clothing loses its edge, particularly as you cannot get up and go for a short walk! Cushions and purpose-made boat seats (that in Fig. 1 attaches to ordinary transverse shelf seats) become decidedly uncomfortable after several hours and the combination of any or all of these problems exacerbates the cramped conditions. Fortunately, with a bit of forethought, these difficulties can be overcome.

The first and perhaps most important consideration is your fishing partner. Bobbing about in a cramped boat for several hours really sorts out a friendship, and many have been strained to breaking point when one party views things differently from the other. The worst source of aggrevation is excessive moving about, standing up and generally rocking the boat; also noise generated by dropping kit on the boards and heavy foot movement. The majority of boat fishing is done at comparatively close range, which really brings home the need for care and quiet. Apart from obvious points like not wearing metal studded waders, the most effective way to deaden noise is to cover the entire bottom of the boat with carpet underlay, and thereafter to move carefully.

If a specially designed boat chair, i.e. one which is clamped to the cross-board, is not available then a picnic chair can be used when fishing static techniques. Otherwise, it will have to be a cushion, foam pad or partially inflated inner tube (not actually as comfortable as some anglers claim).

Everything should be prepared before launching, especially tackling up, and all unnecessary gear, such as umbrellas and rod rests, left in the car. Essential items, like food, spare tackle, etc., should be stored beneath a canvas at one end of the boat, preferably the bows, where they are under the charge of the angler seated nearest to them. Only one landing net is needed, which can either be hooked over a rowlock as in Fig. 2 or, if it is a circular frame, attached to a 2-ft handle stowed under the gunwales. A purpose-made boat rod rest (see Figs 3 and 4) keeps the rods out of the boat and leaves a surprising amount of room, which can be further improved, if it is possible, by removing the middle cross-board (the one the rower uses) and laying it under the gunwales.

## Boat Rod Rest

Boats used on inland waters usually offer cramped enough conditions even without two anglers aboard. This situation is further aggrevated if the rods are placed across the gunwales in the usual fashion. In Figs 3 and 4 we show an easily made boat rod rest which, in addition to freeing space inside the boat, places the rods entirely outside the gunwales, and yet they are still immediately accessible (commercially made models are also available).

The function of this rod rest is self-explanatory. However, we should mention that the V-shaped fork is placed outwards; the inverted U prevents the rod from tipping over the side. The G-clamp is clamped to the gunwale rail and holds everything in place.

Reaching the swim, which could be a mile from the boat yard, staithe or fishing lodge, is achieved by rowing or using an outboard engine. You must always carry oars, in case of emergency, and during fishing these, too, are stored under the gunwales. When in use, however, a secure method of 'fixing' them to the gunwales is needed. Fig. 5 shows the common rowlock, which is located through a metal sleeved reinforced hole in the gunwale and held in place with a split pin. As efficient as rowlocks are, we feel that thole pins (see Fig. 6) are actually an improvement as the oars are effectively bolted to the boat. The pin is passed through a bracket on the gunwale and is then located in a hole through the oar. A nut holds everything in place.

Outboard motors are an invaluable aid to reaching distant spots and at the same time are an important safety aid in the event of a sudden worsening of the weather when a quick run for cover is called for. Seagulls, legendary for their plodding ability and overall reliability, are perhaps the best known petrol-driven motor, but there are numerous alternatives. Electric outboards (see Fig. 7), though generally less powerful, are silent-running and so offer clear advantages: they are ideal when stealth is called for on approaching a swim, especially in shallow water. With the electric motor comes a large battery (ensure it is fully charged!) and this is something else to find space for! It is, of course, an excellent outboard to use for trolling.

It is all very well having something powerful to get you to the fishing area but you will also need something to hold you in place when you get there. If you are fishing a muddy bottomed mere, or a heavily silted broad, for example, a mud-weight (see Fig. 8) is far superior to a conventional anchor. A 2–5 litre paint can, filled with concrete, on a heavy rope is quite sufficient. If the boat still drags on the wind, either let out more rope or tie a length of chain between the mud-weight and the end of the rope, or, add a second weight about a yard away from the first one. Ideally, use a mud-weight at each end of the boat.

A second method of holding steady is to drive two

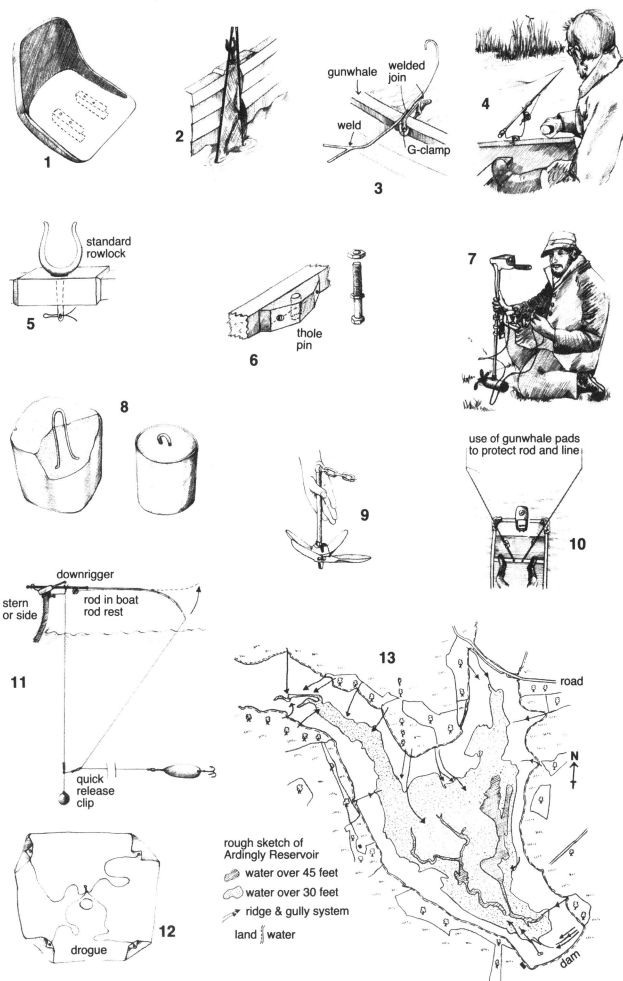

**1**

**2**

**3** gunwhale | welded join | weld | G-clamp

**4**

**5** standard rowlock

**6** thole pin

**7**

**8**

**9**

**10** use of gunwhale pads to protect rod and line

**11** downrigger | stern or side | rod in boat rod rest | quick release clip

**12** drogue

**13** rough sketch of Ardingly Reservoir

water over 45 feet

water over 30 feet

ridge & gully system

land ∫ water

road

N

dam

long wooden stakes into the bottom, at each end of the boat. Although this creates more of a problem if the pike is fighting under the boat, the system does hold the boat far steadier than the mud-weight on a rope. One difficulty is removing the stakes after fishing: they are always more firmly rooted than you think.

The ordinary tined anchor in Fig. 9 is probably more familiar to most anglers and is better used on firmer bottoms, gravel, etc.

A word or two about mooring. With two anglers in the boat and only a light wind and gentle chop, mooring broadside to the wind is quite acceptable and gives an equal vista to both anglers, both up *and* down wind, and across. In a heavy chop this arrangement will cause the boat to pitch a lot and eventually to drag its mooring. If one anchor shifts position more than the other, the boat will swing annoyingly and make bite detection awkward.

Mooring broadside requires co-ordinated actions from both anglers: the boat is rowed into the wind, then slowed and the stern anchor lowered. Once tethered at one end, the wind will begin to push the bows broadside; with some gentle paddling to slow the swing, the bow anchor is lowered just before the required final position. As the anchors take hold the boat should settle where needed.

With only one angler aboard in a strong wind the boat will remain more stable if moored bows into the wind. You may need to pay out more rope to hold position (or use the double weight), while the stern anchor is optional depending on whether or not a swinging boat concerns you. Moored like this it is important to keep the baits further apart, and even use heavy leads to hold position. It is best to keep one rod on each side of the boat (see Fig. 10). Casting one bait further away from the boat than the other will also help keep the lines apart.

Landing pike from the bank and boat is covered on **pages 60–4**, and livebait trolling on **page 42**. Deep water trolling creates the additional problem of keeping the bait or lure down, because the forward movement of the boat lifts the line high in the water. Using lead core lines is one way of keeping the bait deep: pay out more line the deeper the lure is required to run. Alternatively, the time-honoured system of the 'down rigger' shown in Fig. 11 can be used. The system is really self-explanatory but it should be emphasised that the rod is held under tension—the tip curved downwards—by the weight, a sudden springing straight signalling a take. It is useful to mark the 'down rigger' line in feet or metres so that when used in conjunction with an echo sounder the correct depth is fished, the weight being raised or lowered accordingly.

Using the wind to drift the boat, trailing the baits out behind is a lovely technique, but in a strong wind the boat may be travelling too fast. A drogue (see Fig. 12) is the answer. As the boat tows the drogue the latter billows out in the water, thereby slowing down the drift much like a parachute.

Boat safety is largely a matter of commonsense but also comes with experience. Listen to experienced anglers and boatmen, and if you are advised not to go out, heed the warning. Do not venture out on a big water in a tiny boat—10-ft fibreglass dinghies and 500-acre reservoirs do not mix. Pay close attention to weather reports, especially if squalls are expected, and run for shelter before the storm arrives. Do not try to ride it out at anchor. Take out a life jacket and wear it, and do not forget a two-pint capacity, or larger, tin to act as a bailer. If the anchor gets stuck on the bottom and the boat is pitching in a heavy swell, cut the rope and attach a buoy if you have time. Finally, make your first few trips afloat with an experienced boat angler.

### Map of the Water

It is obviously not essential to map out a water, but once completed it does remove much of the hit-and-miss approach so common on big waters. A boat also makes a considerable contribution to fishing successfully 100 acre or more waters, and is essential—with an echo sounder, if possible—to the completion of the map. Our map in Fig. 13 is of Ardingly Reservoir, a water of 180 acres, and shows not only depth contours, gulleys, ridges, shallows and deep holes, but also important landmarks like meadows and woods. The latter are especially useful to line up gulleys against markers on the far bank, and to give a fair idea of where sheltered, and rough, water will be when the wind is in a particular quarter.

As results come along the sensible thing is to plot the captures on the map, perhaps with a colour key to show the month of capture and may be the time of capture. In so doing a picture of pike migration is built up. For example, it could show a movement towards the shallows in early spring and a migration to the 30 ft contour in severe winter weather.

# PROTECTIVE CLOTHING

Although there is no reason why you should not pike fish in the summer, essentially piking is a winter pursuit, and winter weather means warm, dry clothing.

Good quality—and 'Helly Hansen' is the very best—thick fibre pile thermal underwear helps keep in the body warmth, but works best if windproofed and insulated top clothing is worn, there being nothing worse than draughts. This latter problem is the reason why many anglers are wearing one-piece inner and outer suits, but the disadvantage here is that if the weather suddenly warms up it is a case of all or nothing being removed! 'Fur'-lined fingerless mittens keep the hands warm and a woollen hat or anorak hood, though optional, keeps the heat from escaping through the scalp.

Dryness is as important as warmth and here we have a problem. The most efficient waterproof materials cannot 'breathe' and cause condensation on the inside, which is acceptable until the temperature drops. Waxed cotton 'breathes' but is waterproof only as long as the wax coating remains intact. However, such clothing is 'cold' and stiffens in low temperatures. Heavy-duty nylon, even when 'proofed', is only showerproof, and rain seeps along the seams, the collar region and the elbows. Some of the very latest synthetic products, such as 'Gortex' and 'Dartex', offer the best waterproof properties and fortunately some manufacturers are incorporating these materials with good quality insulation like 'Thinsulate'.

Foot protection has been greatly improved in recent years and there is now no problem with cold or wet feet. Waders with heavily cleated rubber soles—not studs—which are a full size larger than normal to accommodate a good pair of insulated socks give excellent general protection, but in severely cold weather 'moon boots', such as the Skeetex brand, are preferable. Though too short in the leg for wading, they afford infinitely better thermal protection than waders. However, in the last couple of years 'Mukluk' thermal waders have come on the market which, teething troubles apart, appear to answer both problems.

Protective clothing for anglers is nearly correct, but still we have anoraks with hoods so small they cover only the back half of the head and sleeves which are too short for anyone of 6 feet in height, and they are often short in the body which means they don't reach the tops of waders! Most hoods also seem to face forwards when you turn your head sideways!

fur-lined thighs of waders

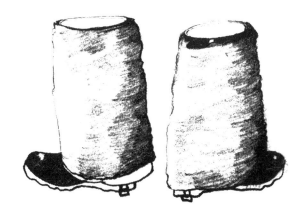

# ECHO SOUNDERS AND FISH LOCATORS

On very large and deep waters, such as the loughs of Ireland and Scottish lochs, it is virtually impossible to depth plumb in the traditional way. The 'Seafarer' echo sounder (see Fig. 1) used from a boat is the only practical way and produces a visual 'bleep' on its circular face dial, indicating the depth directly beneath the boat. The reading is obtained from a sensor head, or transducer, which is lowered over the side of the boat and fixed firmly to the gunwhale in either of the two ways shown in Figs 1a and 1b. In addition to indicating the depth, the 'bleep', depending on how positive it is, gives an idea of the type of bottom present. In Figs 1c and 2–4 we show the readings to be expected over hard bottoms, progressing through to soft silt.

The Eagle Lowrance graph recorder is substantially more sophisticated in its design and the reading it produces. As the name suggests, this instrument produces a printed graph which details not only the depth (in a topographic way) but weedbeds, snags, shoals of fish and individual large fish, too.

However, it is not just a matter of rowing across the water and reading off the information. It is necessary to understand why fish produce different marks on the graph. There are several factors to consider: the speed of the boat, whether the fish is swimming or resting in 'mid water', in which direction it is swimming, and its position within the 20 degree collection 'cone' of the transducer. It is, therefore, not certain that a large mark shows a large fish, although it often does. The perfect mark is obtained when the boat passes slowly over a stationary fish, and takes the form of an elongated, inverted 'V'. The outer edge of the transducer cone picks up the fish and the graph mark will begin to climb as the echo gets stronger. The high point is recorded in the centre of the cone, and the mark then declines as the signal weakens. Pass over the same fish much faster and the read out is much smaller. Pass over a large shoal of fish at speed and the mass of signals fuses together to produce a 'cloud' on the graph.

Not all marks are fish, of course, and it soon becomes evident that a large variety of marks can be recorded. For instance, the instrument can also pick up algae and clouds of daphnia!

With Figs 2, 3 and 4 we are able, thanks to the kindness of Colin Dyson, to describe a variety of readings.

Fig. 2: a vast shoal of fish, probably several different species, recorded in a lake near Amsterdam. Larger fish are lower in the water and smaller ones are nearer the surface. Despite such obviously large numbers of fish, nothing was caught.

Fig. 3: a recording taken at American trolling speed (quite fast) on Lake Michigan. The recorder was adjusted to scan the top half in 60 feet of water. Long vertical marks are most likely to have been made by steelheads.

Fig. 4: another Lake Michigan recording. A fish has lanced upwards to strike near the surface from around 37 feet, just as the trolled lures came along at the original depth of the fish before it struck. The parallel marks are made by the downrigger lead to which the lure is attached. The lure should be set to run at around 60 feet behind the downrigger line.

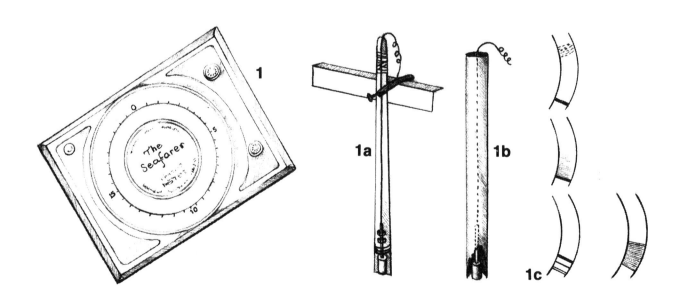

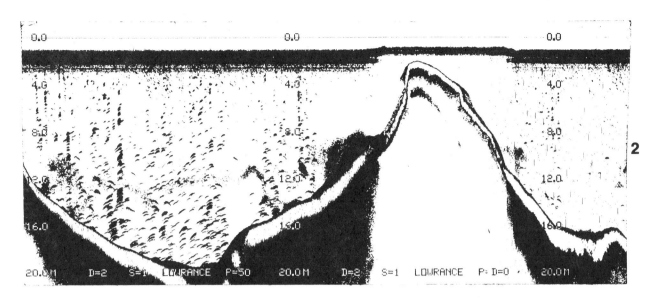

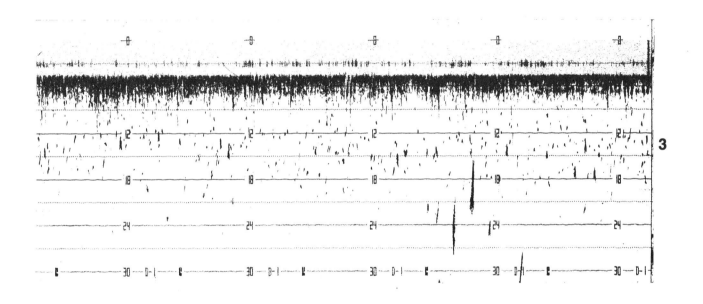

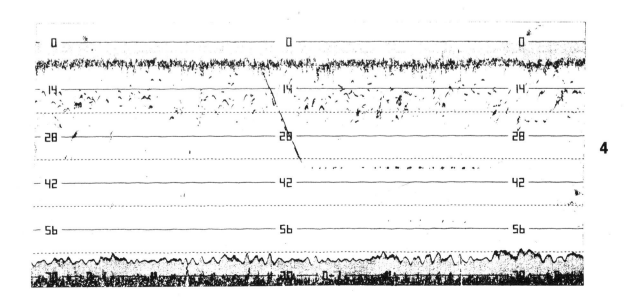

# PLAYING, UNHOOKING
# AND RETURNING

There are no hard and fast rules when playing pike, although it is to the benefit of the pike to land it as quickly as is reasonable, and you do this by making full use of the tackle strength and by, in effect, bullying the fish to the net. This serves two purposes: (1) the pike is landed while it is still fresh, since it can be harmful to return an exhausted fish; and (2), the pike pulls back harder than if you dally, so giving you a harder, though shorter fight.

If the fish leaps, no matter at what distance, keep the line tight. Do not dip the rod tip; keep in firm contact all the time. If the pike dives, especially in the vicinity of snags, lower the rod top close to the surface and over to one side. This will have the effect of swinging the fish back towards the surface and away from danger. Pike which are kiting on the surface are slightly more difficult to deal with because laying the rod over and pulling against the swimming direction of the fish tends merely to cause its mouth to open further and to slow down the process. The best move, whenever possible, is to walk along the bank towards the pike and get a direct head-on pull.

As soon as the pike is within 3 or 4 yards of the angler and if its size warrants a net, sink the landing net (see Fig. 1). By keeping the rod well bent, wait just long enough for the fish to tire sufficiently for you to guide or pull it over the net. When half to two thirds of the fish is over the frame, lift the net to engulf it.

Once on the bank (see Fig. 6) or in the boat, and away from the water's edge, lay the fish on something soft—grass or an unhooking mat. In a boat place the carpet underlay on the boards before even starting out, or keep the fish off the boards. On the bank pre-arrange a suitable spot before the first run comes. Control any movement of the fish to prevent damage and get down immediately to remove the hooks. The unhooking kit should be readily at hand, along with the balance and weighing sling.

There are several well documented approaches to unhooking pike which involve gags, long-nosed pliers, laying the fish on its back and pulling on its lower jaw to open its mouth. We have used each of these methods and have rejected all but one. The method we use, and will describe here, has been proved on several thousands of pike over the last one and a half decades or more. It is safe for the pike and the angler, is quick and is extremely efficient. And it can be used both for jaw-hooked and throat-hooked (or deeper) pike.

With the pike lying still, slide the first two fingers of your hand inside the gill cover and between it and the outside gill raker. Move the fingers to the extreme tip of the jaw and lift the head clear of the ground (with pike up to low double figures). Then lift the entire fish, which has the effect of opening the mouth and flaring the gills. Sometimes at this point the fish may struggle; if it does, lay it down, control any struggles, then start again when all is quiet (see Figs 3 and 4).

If the hook is in the jaw or just inside the mouth, insert a straight pair of forceps through the mouth, clamp the forceps on the hook shank and push down and out. If the hook is further towards the throat, pull on the trace gently to keep everything tight, and either hold the trace swivel between the teeth or get an experienced mate to pull on the trace. Insert the closed forceps between two of the gill rakers, clamp on to the hook shank and turn it upside down. A bit of 'jiggling' and the hook will pop free. In the unfortunate event of the hook being out of sight, but the length of the trace indicates by only an inch or so, pull just a little harder on the trace until the hook shank emerges, and repeat the hook inversion stage (see Fig. 5).

Once the hook is free, release the forceps, close them, and withdraw them through the same path through the gill rakers. Once clear, pull the trace and hooks out through the mouth. With experience this job takes just a few seconds.

If the fish is to be weighed, the safest and surest method is to use a long, closed ended weighing sling which has been wet, shaken, and zeroed on the scales before the fish is inserted. When weighing has been completed the fish can either be returned immediately or retained for just a few moments more for a photograph. Support a double-figure fish with one hand under the chin (see Fig. 6); for larger fish use both hands, one under the jaw, the second under the body in the pelvic region. Hold the pike close to the body and low to the ground, and if it struggles hold it against your body to make certain it is not dropped. Carry it quickly to the water's edge, lowering the body into the water first, followed by the head (see Fig. 2). Support the pike gently until it regains strength and swims powerfully away.

If, due to a long fight or too long out of the water, the pike rolls on to its side, support it in an upright position with rod rests on each side of its body until its strength returns. Do not hurry this operation: allow the pike all the time it needs and even then do your utmost to prevent it from swimming into bankside weed which might block its progress. Stake the pike out in calm water.

One or two words of caution about deeply hooked or badly hooked pike. With today's small hooks little damage is usually caused, but problems can occur. If the hook is tangled with a gill arch, take special care not to cause bleeding. If bleeding does start, get the fish back into the water as quickly as possible where the bleeding should stop quickly. Pike which bleed from the gills *do not die*. Hooks out of sight down the throat are only likely to cause damage if they pierce the gut wall and puncture an organ, which is unlikely if the hooks are small. If gentle pulling does not bring them into sight, cut the trace as close to the presumed position of the hooks as possible and, again, get the pike back into the water quickly. There is plenty of evidence to suggest that this practice does not prevent the fish from feeding as long as the *hooks are small.*

Do not poke about.

Clearly, a deep-seated hook is caused by too long a delay in striking and there is no excuse for it happening *twice.* Always strike quickly; 20 seconds is normally plenty long enough and will usually result in well-hooked pike.

unhooking grip: fingers press against gill cover, *not* gill filaments

ideally the bottom boards should be covered in sacking

# LANDING PIKE

There is no good reason why a gaff should be used to land a pike. Landing nets of adequate size are readily available and should be used at all times when hand-landing is difficult or inadvisable, e.g. when fishing from well above the water. The principles of netting pike are the same as for any other fish, except that being long and thin pike are usually 'folded' into the net. When the pike is thought ready for netting (i.e. when it is *tiring*, not tired, and close to the rod), the net is submerged and angled downwards. As the fish comes over the frame, at least one third, and preferably more, of the net is lifted and 'scooped' to engulf it. Simply remain calm and unhurried, and if the pike rolls off the frame and starts another fight, put the net down and await another opportunity.

As soon as the pike is safely in the mesh pull the whole thing to the bank and carry it well away from the water. It is important to take the weight of the pike off the frame, which would otherwise collapse with a big fish. This can be done in one of two ways. The first and most often recommended is to support the frame with both hands, while one hand still holds the rod. The frame and mesh can also be gathered in one hand so that the pike is supported entirely in the mesh. The alternative method, and one much preferred, is to carry the net and pike in one hand by holding the handle vertically, with the net down. The weight of the pike is thus pulling directly downwards on the handle.

Carry the net, the pike and the rod away from the water's edge to soft, rubble-free grass. Remove the pike carefully from the folds of the net, ensuring that there are no hooks caught in the mesh, and unhook it. On reservoir banks, in boats or other sites where grass banks are not present, lay the pike on a soft mat of carpet underlay, or on an E.T. unhooking mat.

Net design is a matter of personal choice, with most anglers going for a large triangular frame. The idea is that a 36–48 inch frame gives a large usable netting area, but in practice this is not the case.

Fig. 1a details our preferred pike landing net, a circular frame 24 to 30 inches in diameter. Fig. 1b shows the frame and net folded away. A 30-inch circular frame has a circumference of 94¼ inches; to achieve a similar surface, or nettable, area with a triangular frame requires an arm length of no less than 56 inches! The only way to improve on this figure, i.e. to reduce the arm length but still retain a useful surface area, is to use a bowed arm frame, but then why not a circular frame?

A straight-arm triangular frame folds away neatly. The three-hinged circular frame is also not difficult to cope with, whereas the bowed-arm 'triangular' frame is most cumbersome.

Fig. 2b shows the problems associated with netting a long fish, especially one which has stiffened, with a triangular frame. Each of the corners is unusable, particularly the two connected by the drawstring which easily gives way under the weight of the pike. A heavy pike balanced across a corner can cause the frame to tip sideways, thereby allowing the fish to roll off. None of these problems occurs with a rigid circular frame, which as we have already said can be used to scoop out an awkwardly positioned fish. In addition, the corners of triangular nets have an infuriating habit of catching up in reed and undergrowth.

However, try as we may to persuade anglers of the benefits of a circular pike landing net, triangular frames are still commonly used. Whatever you choose, a pole 5 ft in length should carry the frame, other than when boat fishing when you will find a 2-ft pole to be much more convenient, and quite suitable.

There is an alternative method for netting pike from a boat which does require a triangular frame. The frame is used without a pole, the arms being held apart by hand and the cord tensioned against the hinge. Naturally, a second angler is needed in the boat, and one who is not 'jumpy' when close to a splashing fish. With the pike ready for netting, the second angler leans out from the boat and holds the frame open with both hands. As soon as the pike is in the mesh the arms are closed and turned once to wrap the mesh around them; the fish is then lifted into the boat. We are not altogether sure there is much advantage in this technique and we prefer to use the short pole. It requires an experienced netsman and one who is not fearful of getting close to the water and to the pike.

Pike can be landed by hand but this is best left to small fish, particularly lure-caught pike *when you know where the hooks are*. The fish is played out more and then drawn close to the bank, with its head out of the water. When within arm's reach, slip the first and second fingers inside the gill cover and up to the point of the jaw, and in one swift movement lift the pike out of the water and away to safe ground. If the fish thrashes, drop the rod and control the pike's movements before attempting to lift it again. The risk of damage to fish and angler is greater using this method, but there are occasions when it is actually more efficient than netting. Never grip the pike behind the head or with the fingers in the eye sockets.

**Weighing Pike**

Quite naturally anglers are keen to know the weight of a good pike, but this keenness must not overrule compassion for the fish. Above all else weighing a pike must be done efficiently, quickly and accurately, and in that order.

In Fig. 3 we show what is actually the quickest method of weighing a pike, although it is potentially the most dangerous. The balance hook, which must be large in gape, of heavy duty metal and blunt, is passed under the gill cover, between it and the outside gill raker, and up to the natural point of the

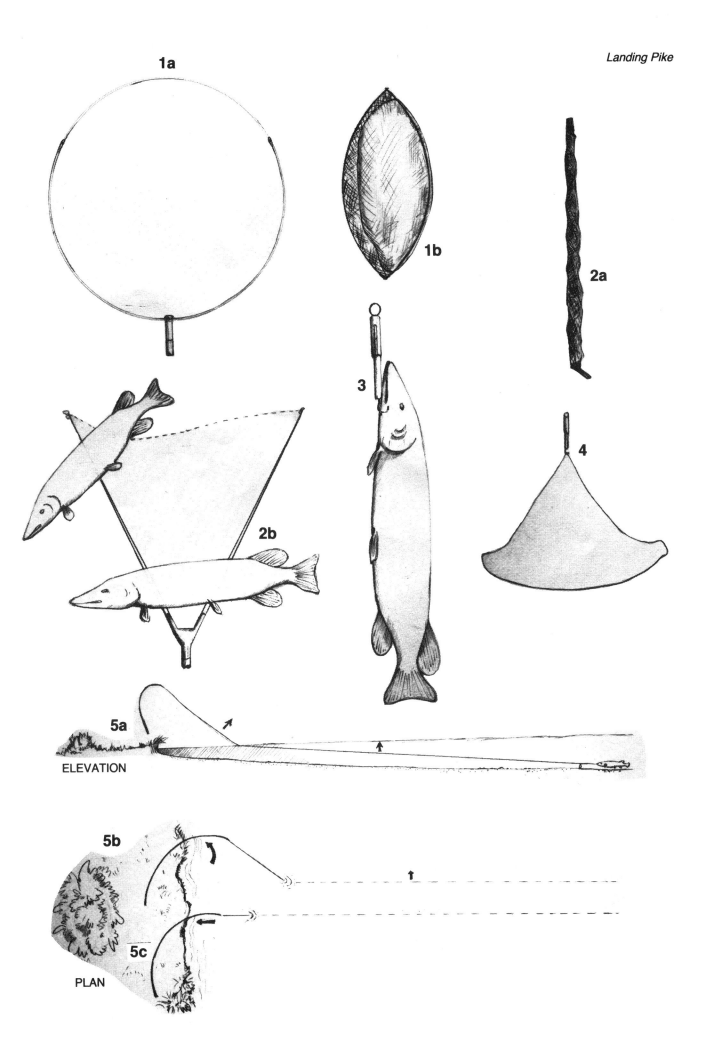

1a

1b

2a

3

2b

4

5a

ELEVATION

5b

5c

PLAN

lower jaw. The fish is lifted carefully and weighed quickly. With the latter point in mind, a tubular balance is better than the Avon-type dial scale which can be confusing to the inexperienced. The danger in this method is the damage which can be caused to the gill rakers if the hook is incorrectly located.

Surprisingly perhaps, we do not condemn this method out of hand, and it is one that we use at times.

Universally more acceptable is the weighing sling shown in Fig. 4. Several independent versions of this sling are available, some with a draw-string, but all are basically the same, consisting of a long nylon 'hammock' which when wetted holds the pike quite securely. A cord drawstring suspends the sling from the balance hook. Providing that the sling is wet, and therefore not slime-removing, and the pike fully contained and protected therein, no harm can come to the fish. However, remember to deduct the weight of the sling or zero the balance against the weight of the sling when weighing a pike. Once again, Eddie Turner must be congratulated for producing a superb weighing sling which is smooth and kind to the fish and weighs very little more when wet than when dry, something which cannot be said of most makes.

If you are a keeper of records then a reliable spring balance is important to document your catches. If you are a seeker of records, especially of pike, then as well as being reliable and capable of reading an unambigious weight it should go up to 50 lb! Personally, we prefer tubular balances, Salters being the best example, because they give one clear reading. Dial balances of the Avon type weigh very accurately but in inexperienced hands can be easily (or deliberately!) misread. Look after your balance, and keep it in a clean dry cloth well away from grit and dampness. You can check the accuracy of a balance by pulling it against two or three other balances. If the readings are the same, it is as accurate as need be.

## Striking

Despite the fact that Martin Gay has probably had more debates with anglers on the 'correct' way to strike a pike run than any other piking topic, successful hooking of pike is really quite easy. The most important thing is to strike on a tight line, although there are other considerations concerning the depth of the water, and therefore the angle of the line through the water and the depth to which the line is sunk.

Figs. 5a–c show the problems diagrammatically, although some explanation is necessary. Firstly, a word about the timing of the strike. Exactly how quickly to strike depends on a number of factors which include bait size, live or deadbait, the number and position of the hooks, the type of run, the size of pike, the mood of the pike on the day, and the water temperature. Large pike can obviously pouch the bait faster than small ones, but do not always do so. Assume that the pike is a good one and that it is quickly pouching the bait. In a nutshell, strike quickly, and always within 20 to 30 seconds irrespective of what the run is doing, and even quicker if the pike is running steadily. 'Fidgety' runs are always the most difficult of which to judge the timing, but do not assume they are small pike.

If the pike is running steadily engage the reel, check the line is not snagged and let the run take up the slack line. Wind quickly until the reel is locked up and strike hard in one continuous upward or sideways movement, all the time ensuring that the reel cannot spin backwards. *Do not* engage the anti-reverse and do not let the clutch slip. If the pike is not running but merely swallowing the bait on the spot, wind up very quickly until the line is dead tight and strike as above. Sometimes the bait is dropped while winding up like this, but not only is there nothing else you can do, we also believe that pike which drop the bait at this time are fish which would have dropped any way.

We cannot overstress the need to strike on a tight line, especially when fishing in shallow water where the strike is effected *along* the water (as strange as that may sound) rather than through it. In deep water comparatively more line is deeply submerged so the angle between the line out of the water and the line submerged creates more resistance, or drag, and thereby reduces the power of the strike. Fig. 5b shows the problem in plan view (Fig. 5a is the side elevation) when the bait is ledgered. There are two ways round this, the first being to strike sideways with the rod parallel to the bank (see Fig. 5c) along the direction of the line, which does not introduce the angle as in Figs. 5a and 5b. The second approach, and the one which we advocate, is to use a float. By keeping the line high in the water, more line is lifted on the strike, thereby reducing that all-important angle.

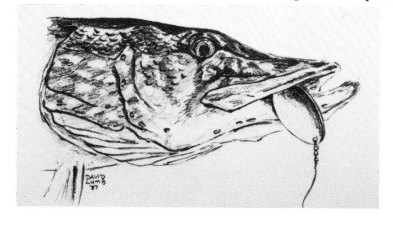

# KEEPING ANGLING RECORDS

Barrie is a veteran keeper of angling records; Martin does so reluctantly because he can see the merits of Barrie's diaries! Having said that, there can be no doubt that a detailed diary maintained on a daily basis, and preferably while actually fishing, can give considerable benefit over successive seasons. How many times have you thought back over the years, recalling the sunny days as a child and the apparently endless successful angling outings? (We all do this because the poor days and the bad weather are eradicated from the memory!)

A diary does not let you forget and, importantly, can point you towards trends, patterns and ultimately answers. Without a diary Barrie and Ray Webb would never have realised the connection between atmospheric pressure and bait preferences. This latter information has proved invaluable ever since its discovery, in the same way that recording facts accurately has left no doubt about feeding spells and how they change as the season progresses, and how individual waters respond to types of weather and water conditions.

Sometimes, of course, there are conflicts, but fishing will never be an exact science, and just as well. However, overall discernible patterns do emerge with considerable consistency, and unless your memory is faultless (and few are) a diary is the only correct way to record the details.

The simplest form of diary is obviously a small hardback notebook carried in the rucksack, in which you jot down notes as things occur on the day, but such diaries (at least Martin Gay's!) usually end up in a mess and hide the real facts. It is much better to have a prepared schedule with itemised sections which are easily followed and even easier to fill in. We offer two such charts. Chart 1 is a sheet completed on the day of fishing, on which as much detail as you wish can be recorded. Chart 2 can be left at home and completed periodically, as long as all the necessary details are recorded each angling day.

However, we would suggest you expand the data collection a little to include daily air temperatures, general weather conditions and, especially important, barometric pressure. In this way, given time and experience, it may be possible to predict trends, and at least make the best of outings a few days hence and aim your bait choice accordingly. Similarly, you will discover waters which fish better in particular conditions and if the weather pattern looks as though it is going a certain way you can choose the venue to suit.

This illustrates a small barometer, which is useful to those who keep records and who wish to investigate pike feeding problems more thoroughly. It is not essential to carry it in the tackle bag, as it can be left in the vehicle. Our diary sheets cater for barometric pressure records.

**Date:** December 20-22 '85    **Venue:** Ardingly Reservoir, Sussex

**Fishing times:** p.m. on 20th; first light - dark, 21st, 22nd.

Additional notes on conditions: Strongish S.W wind, but not a mild wind; somewhat dark and overcast on 21st, calmer towards dusk on both 21st and 22nd.

Target: Pike. The reservoir was to open for coarse fishing on Jan. 1 and Colin Simpson had invited Colin (Dyson), Martin and myself down to give it a try prior to the opening; and to discuss plans.

Catch: One beautiful pike of 11¾ lbs (two sizeable brown trout followed in Gordon Burton brass spoon, but all fish ignored the buzzers) Bait was smelt (cadged from Colin).

## THE DAY / NIGHT

Colin and I stayed at "The Greyhound" in Ardingly village. Excellent old world pub, very friendly (even offered to get up extra early and do breakfast). Afternoon of 20th recce by Colin and I with echo sounder. Found plenty of water over 40' and one hole of 60'+ (seems unlikely, but could be old quarry). Boat sank towards evening! Vandals had loosened the keel bolts. We just got out in time. No joy on 21st. Tried Balcombe Arm, also bank there. Saw one huge pike strike off jetty, flattening water for 5 yards. Baited up off jetty at dark with groundbait laced with pilchard oil and chopped up deadbaits. Fished at end of this trail next morning and fish came at 8 a.m. approx. Only ten yards out, but in 25' of water. No further runs. Martin and Colin fished off dam and, later, from jetty.

### CONCLUSIONS, THOUGHTS etc.

For no good reason didn't like the weather - perhaps the definite chill. Water beautiful and will go again, often. From what we saw and heard it looks like the classic situation where the pike have not been interfered with - namely some big fish, but not hoards of jacks (we'ed have picked them up whatever the conditions). They seem to be no trouble to trout fishers & if there really are 350 lbs coarse fish to the acre then I doubt if they eat many trout, except eye-fluked rainbows perhaps. Must do map.

*devised by Barrie Rickards & Martin Gay*

**Chart 1**

Date: .........................................     Venue: ...............................................................

Fishing times: ...........................................................................

Additional notes on conditions:

Target:

Catch:

THE    DAY / NIGHT

CONCLUSIONS, THOUGHTS etc.

*devised by Barrie Rickards & Martin Gay*

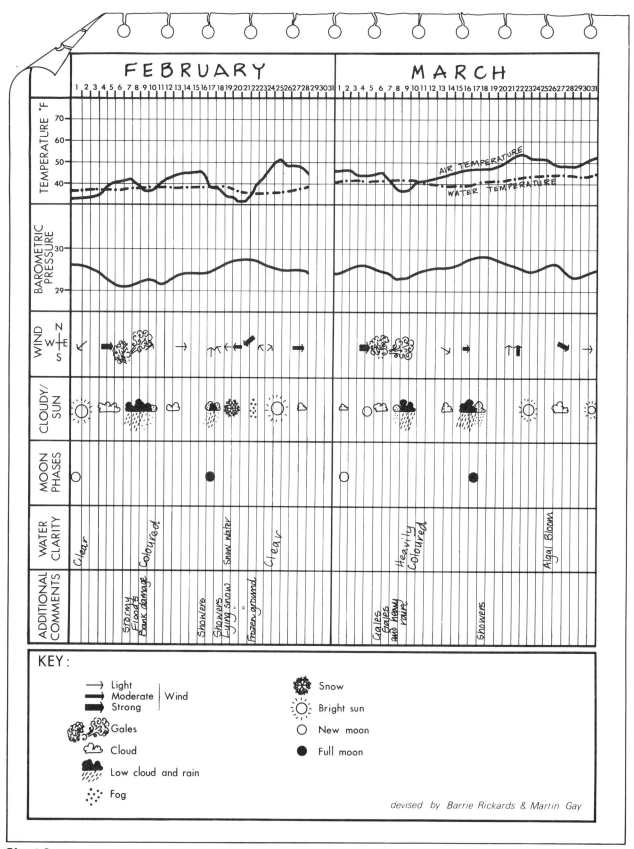

Chart 2

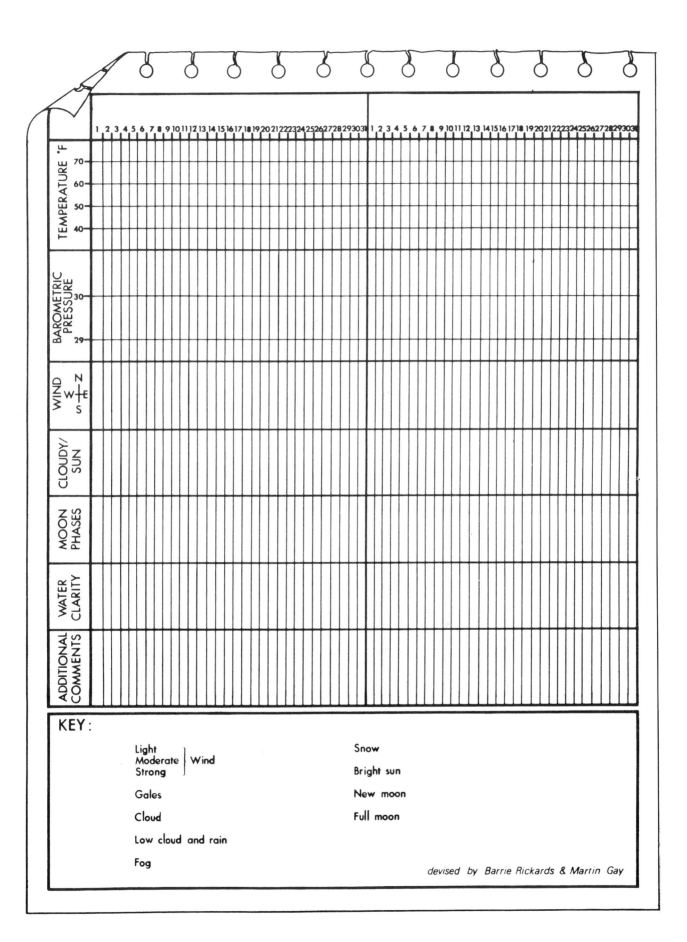

KEY:

Light
Moderate } Wind
Strong

Gales

Cloud

Low cloud and rain

Fog

Snow

Bright sun

New moon

Full moon

*devised by Barrie Rickards & Martin Gay*

# INDEX

# Out in Front

Over the past two seasons the ML3.5 has firmly established itself as the optimum reel for fishing baits at long range. Its wide, big-capacity spool will take up to 250 yards of 12 lb line, yet with a weight of under 11 ozs, the ML3.5 perfectly complements the latest generation of lightweight carbon rods.

There are three other models in the ML series and together with the ML3.5 they form a range of reels to satisfy the requirements of every specialist angler. All four possess carbon bodies, rotors and spools resulting in less weight and greatly increased resistance to corrosion.

Other features boasted by the superb ML series include high-speed retrieve, instant-release spool, free-running aluminium-oxide line-roller, ambidextrous and internal automatic/manual bale-trip mechanism.

| Model | Weight | Line Capacity | Gear Ratio | Suggested Application | Retail Price |
|-------|--------|---------------|-----------|----------------------|--------------|
| ML 1 | 7 | 290 yds/ 4 lbs | 5.1:1 | Chub, Roach | £29.50 |
| ML 2 | 8.5 | 190 yds/ 8 lbs | 5.1:1 | Chub, Tench Barbel | £35 |
| ML 3 | 10.4 | 220 yds/ 12 lbs | 4.5:1 | Carp, Pike | £35 |
| ML 3.5 | 10.8 | 250 yds/ 12 lbs | 4.5:1 | Carp, Pike (Long range) | £36 |

For the name of the Ryobi Masterline stockist in your area, simply telephone **Tewkesbury (0684) 299000**. All "Masterdealers" have been supplied with the 1986 Ryobi Masterline full colour catalogue, but anyone experiencing difficulty in obtaining a copy should send a S.A.E. to **Ryobi Masterline Limited, Cotteswold Road, Tewkesbury, Gloucestershire GL20 5DJ.**